BEYOND THE COLOR LINE

Beyond the Color Line: Pan-Africanist Disputations

Selected Sketches, Letters, Papers and Reviews

BY
Kwesi Kwaa Prah

Africa World Press, Inc.

P.O. Box 1892
Trenton, NJ 08607

P.O. Box 48
Asmara, ERITREA

Africa World Press, Inc.

P.O. Box 1892		P.O. Box 48
Trenton, NJ 08607		Asmara, ERITREA

Copyright © 1998   Kwesi Kwaa Prah

First Printing 1998

Cover design: Jonathan Gullery

Library of Congress Cataloging-in-Publication Data

Prah, K. K.
    Beyond the color line : Pan-Africanist disputations : selected sketches, letters, papers, and reviews / Kwesi Kwaa Prah.
        p. cm.
    Includes bibliographical references and index.
    ISBN 0-86543-629-0 (cloth). – ISBN 0-86543-630-4 (paper)
    1. Pan-Africanism.   2. Africa--Politics and government.
    I. Title.
DT32.5.P72 1997
320.54'9'096–dc21
                                                    97-40970
                                                    CIP

Dedicated to the African youth who will live to fight for the Second Independence.

Table of Contents

Acknowledgements

I thank the *Weekly Mail (Nairobi)*, *Africa Development (CODESRIA - Dakar)* for allowing the reproduction of the texts which first appeared under their auspices.

I would also like to thank *Dorothy Van Kerwel*, who did the typing of most of this manuscript, and *Julian Johnson* who assisted with the computer typesetting of the text.

Kwesi Kwaa Prah
Cape Town. 1996.

Biographical Sketch

In a pre-publication review of this text it was suggested that;

> ..... to publish this book, it must be accompanied by a biographical
> sketch of the author that contains more details than is usually the
> case with biographical notes on dust jackets. Such biographical
> information has great relevance to the contents of the book, since the
> author is a Pan-Africanist of note - an activist in that movement
> rather than a mere scholar of the movement.

I am therefore drawing attention to a few points which may help the
reader to situate this text in the context of my life. I was born in
Kumasi, Ghana on the 20th of December 1942, but grew up largely
in Accra in relatively privileged circumstances. As primary school
children we grew up in the heady days of the independence
movement, and learnt to admire Nkrumah long before we properly
understood the implications of his work. In the company of school-
mates we used, for a period, to regularly at afternoon breaktime, at
three to be precise, go to the roadside and wave at Nkrumah in his
black Opel car on his way to the parliament. We new he meant great
things for the Gold Coast, but precisely what, we had no clue. When
Kenyatta at the time of the Kenya Emergency was imprisoned, we
made heroic songs about him, based on both fact and fiction. Later at
Achimota School other friends, like Kwesi Haizel and Bob Bannerman
were directly involved with journalistic work in support of the African
freedom movement. We were aware as teenagers of the presence in
the country of figures like Kamuzu Banda, George Padmore, Frantz
Fanon, Ras Makonnen and W.E.B. Du Bois. Padmore did not live
very far from where we lived. Pan-Africanism was in the air, and
Joshua Nkomo, Robert Sobukwe, Nelson Mandela, Kenneth Kaunda,
Felix Moumie, Patrice Lumumba, Milton Obote, Haile Selassie,
Tubman, Azikiwe, Awolowo and others became familiar signposts in
our mental map of African politics.

At nineteen, I went off to the Netherlands to study in Leiden, where

I spent six years before moving on to Amsterdam. In Amsterdam, in my house -Keizersgracht 351- I provided space for the Medical Committee Angola which was supplying medicines to the Popular Movement for the Liberation of Angola (MPLA). In Europe towards the end of the 1960s, at the time I was teaching at Heidelberg University, I was elected Secretary-General of the Ghana National Students Organization (GHANASO) which was the Nkrumahist wing of Ghanaian Youth, and which had emerged as the exiled remnants of the Student's Movement (NASSO) hounded out of the country in 1966 after the coup. We managed to unite the movement in exile from Moscow to New York and were able by 1972 to reintegrate the formation with the then existent home base.

I returned to Ghana in 1974. While in Ghana, one of the things we managed to do was to set up a group which placed exiled Zimbabwe kids in schools. We provided also some resources to the South West Africa Peoples Organization (SWAPO) representation in Accra. I left Ghana again in 1976, when it became clear to me and some friends that the then military regime would sooner or later act to confine me. I left Ghana in early May, 1976 under the auspices of the Pan-African Congress of South Africa for Dar Es Salaam. By then I had received an appointment with the University of Zambia (UNZA). I went to Zambia, and briefly settled, only to be advised that I had received appointment in Botswana which was closer to the front against apartheid. So I went to Gaborone, where I taught in the University, but operated underground in various activities, including gun-running on behalf of the African resistance in South Africa. Indeed, at a certain point in the late 1970s, my house was the armoury of the Pan-African Congress of South Africa in Gaborone. I left Botswana in 1980, and after a Visiting Professorship and lecture tour of China, I ended up in Cambridge, England, as a Nuffield Fellow in Darwin College. In 1982 I went to the Sudan to teach in Juba University in the south of the country, but soon became involved in intelligence activity on behalf of the African resistance against Arabisation. Together with some friends we were monitoring Sudanese Army troop movements between the East-bank and the West-bank of the Nile.

This is a loose sketch of my engagement with the movement for African freedom.

I have never supported a discriminative position between African Liberation Movements fighting for the same cause, and have always understood that in South Africa for example, Pan-Africanists can be found in the African National Congress, the Pan-African Congress of South Africa, and the Azania Peoples Organization. I have never believed that the Sudan People Liberation Movement (SPLM) is the sole vehicle to African freedom in the Sudan. I have had less intense but principled linkages with the struggle for freedom in Eritrea.

Beyond Africa I have actively supported the Indonesia Committee in the Netherlands, for whom I provided space in my house, and was part of the solidarity movement against fascism in Chile. I was close to the Dutch Provo Movement, particularly Rob Stolk and Robert Jasper Grootveld.

I have, so far, throughout my life, been committed to the struggle for African emancipation both on this continent and in the diaspora. It has helped to provide meaning to my life and anchor in difficult times. Above all, I need to point out that, for me, in theory and practice, African emancipation can and must contribute to the emancipation of humanity as a whole, it cannot be meaningfully constructed unless it is in harmony with the overall march of humanity towards greater freedom.

Preface

Amongst those who make their business matters related to the future of Africa and her peoples, Pan-Africanism remains a central definitional position on the basis of which social and practical solutions are sought. Its relevance has in recent years assumed greater significance in view of the realisation by many that the narrow *etatisme* of the past twenty five years or so of postcolonialism or neocolonialism, has failed to provide a viable basis for development. As the oldest strand in modern African nationalism, Pan-Africanism is rooted in the late 19th century. Its primary object is the emancipation of African people both on the continent and in the diaspora. In order to achieve this, it specifies African unity as the means to that end. In reaction to the murder of Patrice Lumumba, Frantz Fanon in matchless style wrote, "Africa's great crisis,... she will have to decide whether to go forward or backward. She must understand that it is no longer possible to advance by regions, that, like a great body that refuses any mutilation, she must advance in totality, that there will not be one Africa that fights against colonialism and another that attempts to make arrangements with colonialism" (1).

What with the hindsight of three decades we can say to Fanon's warning and lamentation is that, by and large, Africa over the period has gone backward, she has even failed to advance by regions, and as for mutilation, she has suffered enough and so much that, the mind boggles at her ability to take such relentless attrition. For the present, Africa appears to have accepted neocolonialism and come to terms with the material and socio-psychological humiliations of the condition.

Because most Africans yesterday and today are black, who have for centuries been oppressed by groups which are white, African resistance to western dominance has tended to reflect black consciousness as a reference point; a colour consciousness which has been particularly acute in those areas where blacks live, with whites in control of political power. Historically, black consciousness is not an autonomously derived mental state constructed as an end in itself.

1

In these areas of white power, white racism and prejudice form part of the hegemonic culture. Here race and class are frequently parallel. Black consciousness is a reaction to the perniciousness of white attitudes to the dark skin. This is why African nationalism particularly in the diaspora and settler-colonial areas has been preoccupied with colour. Colour has been consistently used for centuries as an instrument of African oppression. While this exploitation and oppression has been primarily economic, the myth of race and colour has been the language for defining and justifying this practice. The language of resistance has in contradiction reflected colour, and will continue to do so for as long as colour discrimination of people of African descent persists. This point has been fingered as far back as 1931 by George Padmore, in his introduction to; *The Life and Struggles of Negro Toilers*.

> The oppression of Negroes assumes two distinct forms: on the one hand they are oppressed as a class, and on the other as a nation. This national (race) oppression has its basis in the social-economic relation of the Negro under capitalism. National (race) oppression assumes its most pronounced forms in the United States of America, especially in the Black Belt of the Southern States, where lynching, peonage, Jim-Crowism, political disenfranchisement and social ostracism is widespread; and in the Union of South Africa, where the blacks, who form the majority of the entire population, have been robbed of their lands and are segregated on Reserves, enslaved in Compounds, and subjected to the vilest forms of anti-labour and racial laws (Poll, Hut, Pass taxes) and colour bar system in industry (2).

Even where political power has in recent decades been transferred from white minorities to wider black power, white elevation and socio-economic privilege ensures the general persistence of the convergence of race and class. In South Africa today, indeed the ultimate test of the new order will be the extent to which it is successful in breaking the inherited historical mould which makes (in Fanon's language) people rich because they are white and white because they are rich. For Fanon the upshot is that "the cause becomes the consequence".

The African elite, as it emerges into privilege, turns its back on its roots. It tends to adopt indiscriminately, all the cultural and social habits of westerners. It accepts the ideology of the primitivism of African culture and removes itself away from its historical belongings. It becomes "white". It implicitly and often explicitly condemns the culture of mass society to damnation and oblivion, and dialectically by this very act, earns the scorn and contempt of those it seeks to imitate and mimic. As a reference group, it invokes and endorses images of black people which rejects the physical structure of blacks in favour of whites.

During the 1960s, when the cry "black is beautiful" went out in imitation of African Americans, on the African continent, it became for example fashionable to grow one's hair as naturally as possible. There was a decline in the attempts by black people to use skin-bleaching creams and the affectation of western accents of speech. Today we are back where we were before the sixties.

All over Africa, both the young and old desperately stretch their hair with hot combs and/or chemicals, skin bleaching is back with a vengeance, worse than we have ever seen. This is inspite of the damning medical evidence of the cancer producing qualities of such concoctions. I have even seen bizarre cases of European-hair wigs bedecking black African heads. I sometimes ask my students what they think of the fact that we do not see, Europeans, Chinese, or Indians struggling to make their hair look African the way we try to look unlike our natural selves. Of course handsome and beautiful people are to be found in all parts of the world and amongst all people, so, when people grow up seeing themselves and their kind as unattractive, and almost every other white person better looking we have a serious problem.

Kids from so-called international schools in Africa (children of the elite) literally refuse to speak their indigenous languages. Everything associated with the west is treated as better than the indigenous. The psychological syndrome of self-hatred has been transferred successfully in our time to the next generation.

I have often made the point that, the African elite is in terms of its

3

implicit mandate as the leaders of African development, "a castrated elite"; they speak but do not hear themselves, they have eyes but do not see. They are like freed slaves who are unable to leave their old master. They reproduce themselves today with the same values and assumptions that they acknowledged during the colonial period. As an innovative class, they are historically doomed.

Few voices from the African nationalist past have been as pointedly scathing, about the mind and antics of the alienated African elite, than Kobina Sekyi. In his *Sojourner*, his indictment of the "anglo-maniac" was uncanny.

> A product of the low school embroidered by the high,
> Upbrought and trained by similar products, here am I.
>
> I go to school on weekdays (excepting Saturdays)...
> I speak English to soften my harsher native tongue,
> It matters not if I speak the Fanti wrong.
>
> I'm learning to be British, and treat with due contempt,
> The worship of the Fetish, from which I am exempt.
>
> I was baptised an infant, a Christian hedged around
> With prayer from the moment my being was unbound.
>
> I'm clad in coat and trousers, with boots upon my feet;
> And *tamfurafu* and Hausas I seldom deign to greet (3).
>
> For I despise the native that wears the native dress
> The badge that marks the bushman, who never will progress.
>
> All native ways are silly, repulsive, unrefined,
> All customs superstitions, that rule the savage mind.
>
> I like civilization; and I'd be glad to see
> All peoples that are pagan eschew idolatry.
>
> I reckon high the power of Governors and such;
> But our own Kings and Chiefs - why they do not matter much!

And so you see how loyal a Britisher I've grown...
I soon shall go to England....
And there I'll try my hardest to learn the English life,
And I will try to marry a real English wife!

J. Ayodele Langley from whose introduction to Kobina Sekyi's *Blinkards* this poem is quoted, observes that; "thus spoke the anglomaniac, the typical West Coast African so often the object of ridicule in European travellers accounts of life in colonial British West African society" (4). In the foreword to the same book, H.V.H. Sekyi, Kobina Sekyi's son, referring to the anglomaniac and the syndrome which characterizes this mental mould suggested that it was "a kind of social epidemic which first appeared along with the missionaries in the lives of our forbears in the eighteen fifties, gathered strength through the rest of the nineteenth century, and raged in the opening decades of the twentieth. It began with the total rejection of African religious belief in favour of Christianity; it went on to the total confusion of Christianity with Christendom". The diagnosis is right, but I would argue that, the roots are much older than the eighteen fifties. J.E.J. Capitein (1717-1747) reflected a similar turn of mind (5). What is however valid is the fact that, before the mid-nineteenth century, it was restricted to very limited coastal pockets of particularly West Africa, to social elements closely attached and related to western activity emanating from the forts and castles which dotted the coast.

If most obviously Africans are mainly black, to some extent for the present and increasingly in future, there will be more and more non-blacks whose cultures will claim, acquire and assume African sources and connections, to the point that they assert an African identity. It is in this sense that Africaness is ultimately colourless. It is beyond colour. It transcends colour. It is indeed more history, and/or culture, and not biology. I however think we are still very far from there.

The struggle for African emancipation makes meaning only if it is situated within the wider global canvass of humanity in its entirety. African freedom and development cannot (rationally with an eye on the social process as a historical process) be conceived in contradiction to the freedom of any other group. It must be conceptually constructed as part of the expansion and consolidation of democracy and respect for human rights. The fact that the overwhelming mass of Africans are amongst the most wretched of the earth makes the emancipation of Africans a crucial part of the global process of empowerment; the acquisition of the instruments for taking decisions affecting one's existence and the environment; the liberation of the creative spirit in humanity at both individual and collective levels of social life; and the development of the forces of production.

I am quite aware of the fact that there are those who insist that humanity does not make progress; that as Arnold Toynbee suggested, the only thing we learn from history is that we do not learn from history. Technological advancement has been with us since the emergence of homo sapiens, indeed culture as a human product is an enduring feature of human society from its earliest beginnings. Steady technological progress has been made from fire-making by rubbing two pieces of wood to the contemporary revolution of the micro-chip. Remarkably, in our time the pace at which technology is transforming the basis of human existence is mind-boggling. But these material advances have not been always matched by an increasingly improving social conscience. The Nazi gas chambers of Hitlerite Germany, the killing fields of Cambodia, and the Rwanda genocide the argument will run, bear witness to the structural atavism of the human condition; the ability to lapse into a barbaric anti-human mentality on a massive scale and programmed fashion is a danger which always remains with us and stalks our progress.

But this does not detract from the fact that our sense of justice, what is wrong or socially unjust, what we cannot do to our fellow men, what rights we have as humans, are better defined today than they have ever been. In our global village of the present, thanks to the technological know-how we have, we are all watching and questioning what we do to each other on a scale larger than we have ever done. So that, even when we degenerate and become bestial and inhumane to each other, at least the voices of sanction and condemnation will express universal opprobrium or revulsion. Sometimes punishment can and is dispensed for man's inhumanity to man. But unfortunately, invariably such punishment is not apportioned as a collective universal responsibility, but rather a prerogative of the self-appointed leadership of the human conscience of our times. Only the dominant powers of today's world have the means and ability to impose punishment in the human community. They claim often a moral highground which their whole history in relation to the rest of humanity cannot, and does not, accord them. In their dealings with the "unfit men and beaten races" of the world, the hypocrisy of the captains of western power defies sober imagination. Thus western moralism has not infrequently been freely and desperately twisted, and made an instrument for the defence of purely selfish western interests and the pursuit of exclusivist *real politik.*

During the closing stages of the colonial epoch, when the colonial empires were being unscrambled, propagandists and imperial ideologues suggested that, they were leaving the colonial territories on their own volition and initiative, and were motivated by the highest moral considerations. This propaganda and intellectual make-believe that was churned out was that, maintaining the colonial empires was a heavy material and human resource burden on the colonial powers. As the argument ran, it was on account of their Christian conscience and concern for the lot of uncivilised humanity that they colonised us in the first place, and were preparing the colonial peoples for self-government. The myth of the "white man's burden" and the "civilizing mission" were ideological forms created to justify an unholy cause. This attitude of claiming honourable intentions where shame is more appropriately due is illustrated by a reference made by Margery Perham in her, *Africans and British Rule.* She wrote:

> A picture in the journal *Punch* of 1894 shows John Bull looking unhappily down at a black baby which has been put in a basket on his doorstep, saying, "What, another! Well, I suppose I must take it in" (6).

Nothing could have been further from the truth. Colonialism at heart was not advised by altruistic, noble or humane considerations. It was attendant on the development of capitalism. The creation of colonial empires and spheres of influence was invariably achieved through the application of brute force and naked violence encouraged

7

by sporadic paroxysms of jingoism and the ethos of "my country right or wrong". In the process in some areas, whole peoples were exterminated. The military campaigns of colonialists, euphemistically called "pacification" involved numerous major and minor wars. From its very beginning, slavery, forced labour, taxation, land appropriation, ruthless exploitation and plunder of resources were the hallmarks of the establishment of colonial power. Where and when the western conscience has been more honest and candid, as was the case with Rita Hinden in her *Empire and After (1949)* the perceptive point was made that,

> There is some sentiment within the human heart which revolts against outside interference in the shaping of one's life. Nations and individuals, alike, share this fundamental emotion... This sentiment hinges on the basic desire of all human beings for self-respect....What self-respecting man allows himself to be dependent on the whims - or even on the goodwill - of another? The trouble about all imperial relationships - even let it be stressed, the most beneficent - is that they infringe the fundamental dignity of the dependent people.

Nowhere in Africa, Asia, or the Americas, did the colonized quietly accept the brutal impositions of the colonial powers. Nationalist reaction to colonialism was an extension of the tradition of resistance against colonial control. I would however draw attention to the fact that, although western cruelties and inhumanities to non-western humanity have been of enormous proportions, the western colonial experience has also, as Marx pointed out in his piece on *The Results of British Rule in India*, introduced modern technological culture into backward pre-industrial societies. The dialectic in history is relentless and inescapable.

If Pan-Africanism is an idea, it is not as an idea that its impact has been most felt. Until 1945, its impact was limited to the western world. The Manchester meeting of that year marked a new era in the history of African nationalism. It was from Manchester that the final call for colonial freedom went out. The Nkrumahs, Kenyattas, the Bandas, the Koinanges, became the contemporary standard-bearers of

African nationalism. It was this generation of leadership which translated the idea into the language of the mass movement and towards political decolonization. But when at midnight on the 5th of March 1957, at the Polo Grounds in Accra, with tears of joy and overwhelming emotion, Nkrumah announced to the teeming crowds that, "Ghana our beloved country, is free forever" little did he know or understand that, he was becoming a leader of only a reformed colonial state. It is easy to change the name of a state, hoist a new flag, and sing to the strains of a new national anthem. It is another thing to sever the hold, and throw off for good, the suffocating embrace of imperialism. The Americans learnt that in their war of independence, the Vietnamese have demonstrated that learning process in our lifetime, the Soviets went through a civil war to comprehend this, and the Chinese took their queue on the Long March and back. The strategy and tactics for these two different objectives are as different as day and night. Thus within a decade of the Manchester Conference, Africa was at the door of neocolonialism. With the advantage of almost forty years of educative history, it is easy to recognize the naivety of some of the early attempts at African unity as exemplified by the November 23, 1958, *Ghana-Guinea Joint Declaration* which opens thus:

> Inspired by the example of the thirteen American colonies, which on the attainment of their independence constituted themselves into a confederacy, which ultimately developed into the United States of America, inspired also by the tendencies among the people of Europe, Asia and the Middle East to organize in a national manner, and inspired further by the Declaration of the Accra Conference regarding the African Personality. We the Prime Ministers of Ghana and Guinea, on behalf of our respective governments, and subject to the ratification of our respective national assemblies, have agreed to constitute our two states as the nucleus of a Union of West African states (7).

The social classes which inherited the colonial powers have a bad record. Creatures of colonialism, they have never been able to live down their heritage. They are trapped and marked by the political and economic conditions of their birth and history, in a way that makes them custodians of an order appendaged in inferiority to the metropolitan powers of the world. They are more, cheaply rewarded guardsmen of dominant interests of the global economy, than representatives of the broader masses of their own societies. They have so little confidence in their own societies that, even when they as is common practice loot the state and treat the public treasury as booty, they invest their ill-gotten gains outside and not in their "booty economies".

The neocolonial state in Africa is destined to die a shameful death, choked by its self-made muck. On the road to that demise, the era of warlordism is upon us. In large areas of East, West and Central Africa today, warlords and brigands terrorize town and countryside by day and night. In parts of these areas like Zaire, Sudan, Somalia, Liberia or Sierra Leone, central governments have ceased to exercise any control over the hinterland. The neocolonial state as a "nation-state" in Africa cannot be saved. Right from the start, it was ill-starred and ill-conceived, it was a crude political contrivance foisted on Africans by the departing colonial powers to maintain continuity in the protection of their interests. It has ran its historical course. Its day is done. Based on the Berlin Conference of 1885 and its subsequent elaborations, it was inherited with modifications at the start of the postcolonial period. Since then, in one country after the other, it has failed miserably as an instrument for sustained development. Rather, military-bureaucratic jackboot-rule tempered by single-party dictatorships have dominated postcolonial Africa's political history.

The era of warlordism represents further collapse of the state. This indeed, is the era we are in. Warlordism thrives on, and encourages localism. For the masses, with a disintegrating centre, narrow localist solidarities become more useful points of reference. Ethnicism and regionalism have increasingly become relevant symbols for existential survival of contending localist elites, as conditions further deteriorate.

Pan-Africanist solutions are the only responses capable of offering Africa a way out of the deepening crisis. Such solutions transcend the afflictions of the colonial experience and treat westernism only as an innovational fund, from which is selected institutional inputs adapted to African historical and cultural conditions. Only a rational, hardnosed, unmystical, unsentimental Afrocentricism free from cant and mumbo jumbo, can turn around the developmental retrogression and cultural stagnation that has quagmired African socio-economic advancement.

The motto of the 7th PAC (Pan-African Congress), "organize don't agonize" was well selected. Too many Pan-Africanists remain intellectual aficionados of the idea. Students who study and write about Pan-Africanists. Pan-Africanism in our times should be largely practice. Practice which rationally engages reality with an object of changing the real world. Pan-Africanism, if it is to successfully confront the challenges of tomorrow should not acquiesce in the rhetorical fantasies of a pseudo-church; a community of "believers" who meet every so many years, to affirm their faith and venerate their ancestry and its iconography. The challenge is to organize democratic institutions for the emancipation and development of mass society. But as a concept, mass society must transcend populism and empty collectivist slogan-mongering, so that notionally and practically Pan-Africanist practice avoids the pitfalls of corporatist or rightwing programming. Mass society as a notion must conceptually differentiate and structurize into its component classes, and programmes must articulate and plan the ascendancy of the more deprived majorities within the constituency. Only then, can it embrace and systematically empower an ever widening constituency.

Pan-Africanism is at the same time an affirmation and assertion of African humanity, a spirit of indomitability, an attestation of the right and willingness of Africans to unite and seize their equality amongst humankind. It is not a dogma cast in stone by a political pedigree, and which requires doctrinal fidelity every time it is called into analytical or practical service. It is a dynamic frame of reference which responds to changes in focus and relevance according to changing historical realities.

This text is a collection of outpourings related to Pan-Africanism as an idea for African emancipation. It is my firmly held view that as a social organizational principle, it constitutes the most plausible position from which a rational approach to the problems of African

11

advancement can be solved. What the post-colonial experience in Africa has proved beyond doubt, is that, none of the states of contemporary Africa is economically and socially viable. Only unity will save Africa.

While the essentials of the idea have historical grounding and can therefore be philosophically traced as an evolved body of views, it must at each historical conjuncture seek meaning through practice and social engagement, in order to test its relevance and competence, as an instrument for social change. It is through practice and experience that its theoretical refinement can be engendered. Like all ideas and methodologies of social change which stand the test of time, it is the ability to evolve and adapt to changing realities which identifies the touchstone of its strategic significance. If Pan-Africanism continuously redefines itself and socially redeems its viability, this is largely within historically recognizable parameters which are indeed the common conceptual terrain of the various contributors to its definition from the 19th century. However, the shared conceptual terrain is not fixed or cast in stone with biblical finality. It is a "commons" to which we add and subtract. Therefore textual canonization or repetition *ad nauseam* of 19th century assumptions as late 20th century gospel for African development constitutes a replacement of rationality with meta-rational sentimentalism. Pan-Africanism must review and renew its intellectual baggage through a critical interrogation of its history and praxis.

The collection presented in this volume is a selection of letters, papers, reviews and biographical sketches, which together provide a window into my thinking on Pan-Africanism and related issues. They are drawn from materials from the 80s and 90s. *Ras Makonnen: A True Pan-Africanist*, is a short appreciation I wrote in Nairobi when Makonnen died on December the 18th, 1983. His modest terrace house close to the main road to the Airport was a meeting point for exiles from all corners of the black world. It was then particularly popular with South Africans. This sketch appeared in *The Weekly Mail (Nairobi)* during the first week of 1984. *The Call for the 7th Pan-African Congress* reproduced here was a draft which was put before the International Preparatory Committee of the 7th PAC at the request of my old friend Bankie F. Bankie. *From a Debating Platform to a*

12

Transformatory Organization: What We Demand of African Governments was a submission made in absentia to the Preparatory Committee Meeting of the 7th Pan-African Congress, Kampala, 9th September 1993. *The Cause Of Our Times: Pan-Africanism Revisited* was written over a period of time. Initially, it was intended to be a response to a letter from Dani Nabudere. Additions and revisions were in time made to it. So, although I presented it to the 7th PAC as a contribution, its originally conceived destination was different. *The Diaspora as Host* spells out an argument and elaborates the need for an initiative which would create the platform for developing relevant theoretical approaches to the practical tasks of Pan-Africanism in the new century, indeed the new millennium. In a way, it was a result of conclusions I reached before the Kampala meeting but which became crystallized and argumentatively cast in my mind during and after Kampala.

Beyond the Colour Line: The Language Of Pan-Africanism and the Pan-Africanism of Language was my presentation in October 1995 to the 50th Anniversary commemoration in Manchester of the 1945 Manchester Congress (the 5th PAC). It articulates issues of current interest in my work both as an academic and an African voice. African languages and their unstinted usage, it appears to me, is the key to African development. This point ties in closely with, the Colloquium I organized in July 1996 in Cape Town on the *Harmonization and Standardization of African Languages for Education and Development* (11th-13th July). *Joseph Oduho, An African Patriot: A Reflection*, is in memory of a friend, one of the unsung heroes of the struggle for African freedom. I owe his memory a longer tribute which is in preparation and should appear in the not too distant future. The piece which appears here was requested by Kwame Karikari, the Ghanaian academic and political activist for a journal he has been planning. *The Tripoli Initiative and the Tasks of the Pan-African Movement Today* was a letter I sent to Tajudeen Abdul Rahim, head of the Secretariat which was set up by the 7th PAC. He had been aware of my opposition to, and questions, regarding the suitability of the Khaddafi regime as host for the next PAC. When we met in Manchester, he suggested that I put my argument on paper. *Digesting Manchester 1995* is a reaction to a draft report I received in July 1996 from Barbara Ransby entitled; *Principles Agreed Upon at the 50th Anniversary of the Pan-African Congress in Manchester. 13-15, October 1995.* I wrote, *Deracializing Afrikanerdom* for the *Pre-Congress Colloquium of the 13th World Congress of Sociology. Bielefeld, Germany. July 15th-18th, 1994.* It was my intellectual response to what I consider to be the legacy of apartheid on African people of different shades of skin-colour of the Cape, in South Africa. The subsequent piece *The Subvention of the Invention of Africa* appeared in *Africa Development* as a review of V.Y. Mudimbe's rich work *The Invention of Africa* (Indiana University Press. Bloomington. Indiana. And James Currey. London. 1988). *Accusing the Victims in My Father's House* is a review of Anthony Kwame Appiah's fascinating text, *In My Father's House* . Methuen. London. 1992. Shortly before this book went to press, this review was published in the *CODESRIA Bulletin* (1997). Collectively these pieces help to define my position in contemporary debates on Pan-Africanism which as I say, is "the Cause of Our Times". Given the separate nature of the pieces assembled here, there are some issues and arguments which are repeated in various ways in the text.

Notes

1. Frantz Fanon. "Lumumba's Death: Could We do Otherwise". In, *Towards the African Revolution*. 1970. p.202-203.

2. George Padmore. *The Life and Struggles of Negro Toilers*. London. 1931.

3. Tamfurafu is in the Fanti dialect of Akan, a person who uses the toga-like piece worn in West Africa particularly along the coast, and the immediately adjoining forest-region areas. Among especially the Fanti it has in the past been associated with "cultural rawness", absence of western education and western sophistication; it has been considered as a likely sign of illiteracy and low social class status. Hausa of course is the name of one of the most illustrious of the West African Sahelian precolonial states. For centuries, itinerant traders and craftsmen from this area have filtered into the south, but during the era of cash crop production and mining, the designation was in the south particularly along the coast used as a generic term for

all northeners in the south, who came to seek employment and livelihood as migrant labourers in the cash economy of the south. Because of their generally lower class status, they tended to be looked down upon by the southerners.

4. See, J. Ayodele Langley. Introduction to, Kobina Sekyi. *The Blinkards.* 1915. 1982 edition. London. 1982. pp.12-13.

5. See K.K. Prah. *J.E.J. Capitein. (1717-1747). A Critical Study of an Eighteenth Century African.* Braamfontein. 1993. Also, Trenton. 1994.

6. Margery Perham. *Africans and British Rule.* London. 1941. p.45.

7. Quoted here from, Alex Quaison-Sackey. *Africa Unbound. Reflections of an African Statesman.* New York. 1963. p.76.

Sudan: The Roots of the Revolt

Appeared in The Weekly Mail (Nairobi), May 4th, 1984.

Going by recent events, the Sudan, Africa's largest country by geographical size, appears to be hurtling inexorably into the fratricidal vortex of another civil war. *(When this paper was first written, the latest instalment of war in the Sudan had just started. It has continued to the present, 1996).* From 1955 to 1972, the south was locked in armed conflict with the dominant north. After 17 years of vicious war, the country settled down to peace after the Addis Ababa Agreement of March 28, 1972, reached through the good offices of the *All Africa Council of Churches* and the late Emperor Haile Selassie. A decade later, peace had become part of history and the Sudanese were back on the battlefield. Why has this happened? What are the roots of the revolt?

It is generally assumed that the Sudan is an Arab country. In actual fact, nothing is further from the truth. According to the 1956 census, the first and last Sudanese census, which gave a count of Arab and African only 38 per cent of the population claimed to be Arabic. The majority of the population is African. The south, which is almost completely Christian and animist, is overwhelmingly African and includes principally the Dinka, Nuer, Shilluk, the Bari-speaking people, the Zande and the Latuka. The north is Islamised but, more importantly, Arabised. But here again the principal groups are non-Arabic. A good proportion of them are descendants of earlier Sudanese natives who controlled the north before the influx of Arab settlers about 600 years ago. Although many of them have accepted Islam generally, they have consistently resisted Arabisation. These groups are mainly the Beja in the north-east, the Fur in the west, who are historically closely related to the ethnicities around Bornu in northern Nigeria, the Messalith and the Zaghawa, also of the west. The Nuba of Kordofan and the Funj of the Ethiopian foothills are principally animists with some Christians and Muslims. Of all the non-Arab groups, it appears that only the Nubians in the north Nile

16

Valley, some of whom are in southern Egypt, have tended in recent decades to deny their Africaness on a significant scale. It is particularly among them that Arabisation has been successful. Prior to being Islamised, and later Arabised, the Nubians ironically were Christians.

While the process of Arabisation first involves the adoption of Islam, it is clearly not the crucial factor, as the situation in East and West Africa clearly bears out. A good proportion of Africans in the east and west are Muslims but do not consider themselves to be Arabs. Arabisation in the Sudan entails the slow but steady effacement of African languages and the adoption of Arab names, customs and general cultural patterns. In the western Sudan today, languages like Tungur, Birgit and Berta are dying out as Arabisation steadily undermines African culture. This process is generally helped by the social ethos of Arab-dominated Sudanese society which regards Arab culture as superior and Africa as *a civilisation vacuum*. This attitude is enhanced and maintained by the fact that the Arab elite in the Sudan has dominated the economy, the bureaucracy and the political and cultural life of society as a whole. This elite was already firmly in place before the departure of the colonial administration. The higher echelons of the Sudanese army are mainly peopled by Arabs and Arabised northerners, while the rank and file is overwhelmingly African.

One factor which has throughout the modern history of the Sudan affected relations between the African majority and the Arab minority is the heritage of Arab slavery in the Sudan. It has been estimated that before the termination of the slave trade in the Sudan, during the 19th century, the population of Africans decreased from eight and a half to two million in a few years due to the ravages of the infamous trade. Africans in the Sudan, particularly in the south, find it ironical that the descendants of these slaves are the ones who have been integrated into Arab society in the north.

The Sudan, like most other African countries, was a creation of European power during the period of the scramble for Africa. The main consideration which decided where the borders of the Sudan should lie was an attempt by the British to keep virtually the whole

Nile Basin intact, for on the river Egypt depended, and Egypt after the Suez Canal was opened in 1869 was strategic for British interests east of Suez.

Before 1820, when the Sudan was invaded by the Turco-Egyptian armies, except for parts of the north close to Arab settlements relatively little contact existed between the African south and Arabs in the north.   Even then, it was only after 1838 that the Turco-Egyptian administration under Mohammed Ali initiated expeditions southwards to gather information.   After that, a succession of mainly European-led explorers pushed steadily south.   By 1877 the course of the Nile was completely known.   Under the Turco-Egyptian regime the slave and ivory trade developed in scope.

In 1847, Turkey suppressed the slave trade, and in 1860 the Khedive of Egypt forbade slavery in Egypt and the Sudan, although in fact the trade grew in intensity.   Between 1869 and 1879, the administration made ineffectual efforts to halt the trade.   British occupation of Egypt in 1882 heralded the introduction of European power into the Sudan.   However, in the previous year, the Madhist revolt had started; between 1881 and 1884 the Mahdists consolidated their power in the south and held on until they were chased out in 1897 by the local tribes and the Belgians.   Under the Mahdist administration, slavery continued.   Mahdist power collapsed at Omdurman in 1898 under the onslaught of Anglo-Egyptian forces. The fight against the slave trade took a new lease on life, and under British rule, Christian missionaries penetrated the south.

The British largely administered the south separately from the north and the "primary pacification" of Africans continued until early in the 1930s.   However, in the late 1940s, Britain for various reasons decided to throw the lot of the south and the north together instead of linking the south with East Africa, as had often been considered since the beginning of British rule.   It appears that the main reason for throwing the lot of the south in with the largely Arabised north was determined by the wish to appease Egyptian interests in the Sudan, in order that in turn British interests in the Suez Canal zone could be assured.

After these decisions had been made, in 1947 a conference was held in Juba, to see how the south would cope with the north within the framework of the same political institutions after the British had left. Although southerners were assured of northern goodwill and intentions, this did not completely remove southern suspicions or allay their fears. Internal self-government came in 1953; in preparation towards this, an Anglo-Egyptian agreement was reached in Cairo with northern contribution but without the south. This exacerbated southern fears. The next serious blow to southern confidence resulted from the 1954 Sudanisation process of the civil bureaucracy. Of the 800 key positions to be localised, the southerners were given only four.

After this, southern demands for federation became as vociferous as they were ineffectual. The whole atmosphere of suspicion and mistrust finally came to a head in August, 1955, when very quietly processes were put into motion to transfer northern troops to the south, as it were to neutralise the southern troops of the Equatorial Corps. A mutiny broke out which historically became the opening shots of the first civil war. Although most of the rebellion was quelled within a couple of weeks, rebels under Latada in the Sudan-Uganda border area continued for almost two years. Another group which operated further west in the Zaire border area under Ali Gbatala has never given up.

When independence came in January, 1956, it arrived with the general understanding and hope that the south would soon be given federal status. This never happened. In November, 1958 the southern problem prompted the military under Gen. Abboud to take over from Abdulla Khalil. Abboud, convinced that if the southerners were Islamised and Arabised they would accept northern tutelage, proceeded with a tough and expensive Islamisation and Arabisation programme in the south. Chiefs who accepted Muslim names and mosques in their areas were rewarded. Muslim schools (Khalwas) were dotted rapidly all over the south. Arabic books were given free of charge, and fees in Arabic schools were non-existent, in contrast to the case, in the English-medium schools. In 1960, a rumour broke out that southern intellectuals were to be purged. This led to the exodus in December of that year into neighbouring African countries

19

of what became the core leadership of African resistance against Arabisation in the Sudan. By 1963, the Anya Nya (guerilla resistance army) had been formed. In 1965, Anya Nya pressure forced the Sudanese government to agree to a round-table conference with the insurgents in Khartoum. The conference failed to reach agreement and the parties went back to the battlefield, with reports a few months later of large-scale massacres of civilians in the south.

After Numeiry came to power in a coup in 1969, conciliatory gestures were made to African resistance, which opened the way to the 1972 agreement. But in 1975, the integration process of the Anya Nya into the Sudanese army broke down in Akobo. This incident saw the beginnings of Anya Nya II. Within a decade of the Akobo incident, the Sudanese government, in addition to a number of acts of legislation and decrees, redivided the south and subsequently imposed Islamic law on the whole country. These moves, according to observers, went against the spirit and letter of the Addis Ababa Agreement, and constituted the last straw for southerners who, particularly in Upper Nile and Bahr el Ghazal provinces, started moving and masse into guerrilla camps, pushing forward the momentum of the second civil war.

As far as the north is concerned, the state and its Arabic character must be maintained. But for the insurgents it appears that the basic issue is the question of whether the African majority of the Sudan will allow the minority Arab elite to Arabise them and bring them fully into the orbit of the Arab world, or whether they will struggle to maintain their African identity.

Ras Makonnen: True Pan-Africanist

An Appreciation: The Weekly Review (Nairobi), January 6th, 1984.

On December 18, 1983, Dr. T.R. Makonnen, an old pan-Africanist front-liner, died peacefully in his house in Nairobi West while being attended to by his two sons, Lorenzo and Menelik. His death brought to a close the struggles of a man who throughout his lifetime worked tirelessly at the expense of his own family life, with other like-minded people, to see that the national aspirations for independence and unity of black people in Africa and the Diaspora could be achieved.

T.R. Makonnen (nee Griffith) was born in Buxton, Guyana, at the beginning of this century, at a time when the aura of bondage and servitude still hung heavily over the blackman. After going through primary and secondary school in Guyana, Makonnen was for a period involved with his father and cousin, David Talbot, in diamond mining. It was at this time that he came under the influence of the ideas of Marcus Garvey.

In 1927, Makonnen went to Texas to study mineralogy. Soon after his arrival he was drawn into YMCA activities through which he made his first important contacts with black people from Africa and laid the foundation for his reputation as a singularly gifted speaker. Makonnen was actively engaged in the raging debates of those days on the comparative merits of the views of Du Bois and Garvey. His collaboration with George Padmore, then Malcolm Nurse, a nephew of Sylvester Williams, also dates from this period.

In 1933, Makonnen moved to Cornell University where he continued his activities as a champion of the cause of black people. He learnt from men like the economist, Scott-Nearing, and the anthropologist, Franz Boas. His brief flirtation with the radical American left during these years, drew in his own words, jocular remarks from the Nigerian, Azikiwe, and the Ugandan, Kalibala, who were also in America at the time. A good number of his generation got their early political education from associations on the left of the political spectrum.

21

It was at about the time that Mussolini unravelled his designs on Ethiopia that the young Guyanan changed his name to Makonnen in order to emphasise his Ethiopian preoccupations. Together with Makonnen Desta, Peter Mbiyu Koinange, Workineh Martin and others, T.R. Makonnen worked to publicise the Ethiopian crisis to sympathetic ears. Indeed, it was partly because of the lack of information on the Ethiopian crisis that Makonnen moved to Europe in 1935, ostensibly to pursue veterinary studies in Denmark. It was on his first brief visit to London - en route to Denmark - that he met and shared a platform with C.L.R. James and Jomo Kenyatta at a meeting in Trafalgar Square on the Ethiopian crisis, organised by the International African Friends of Ethiopia (IAFE).

For political reasons and circumstances surrounding his protestations in Denmark about the Ethiopian question, Makonnen was, after a sojourn of two years, deported to Britain. On the boat, he met Paul Robeson who had then left America and was establishing a name for himself at the Unity Theatre in London. Their meeting opened up possibilities of collaboration in efforts towards the achievement of black freedom.

When Haile Selassie went into exile in Britain, Makonnen, Kenyatta, Wallace-Johnson and others organised a group to welcome him.

At the outbreak of the second world war, Makonnen, helped by Peter Milliard, moved from London to Manchester, where he successfully established a chain of restaurants. The profits from his efforts were largely pushed into their Pan-Africanist schemes. Perhaps the most historically significant of these efforts was the Fifth Manchester Pan-African Congress and the allied Pan-African Federation Press. His association with Nkrumah (Ghana), Peter Abrahams (South Africa) Fadipe (Nigeria) and Du Bois developed during this period. During the post-war years, Makonnen worked with members of the Somali Youth League in Britain to improve Somali-Ethiopian relations.

Makonnen was one of the last people to see Kenyatta before he left Britain to return to Kenya. Indeed, years later when Kenyatta's arrest was imminent, Makonnen was questioned in Britain by the MI-5 about his contacts with Kenyatta. His political contacts and activities at this time also included work with the Sudanese Umma, and in particular with men like Abdalla Khalil Bey and Mohammed Mahjoub.

The struggle for independence in Africa emerged in earnest during the 1950s. When, in 1956, independence came within reach in Ghana, after a preliminary visit, Makonnen went to settle there. Initially, he worked with Padmore as an adviser on African affairs, subsequently moving to the newly-established African Affairs Centre as director. It was in this latter capacity in the late 50s that he came into contact with Kaunda, Lumumba, Roberto, Nkomo, Banda and other leaders of African opinion. As he used to say to Nkrumah: "I am at your beck and call. If you want me to go to Central Africa, or to go to Nyerere or Obote to take the message, then let me go. That's my job".

Makonnen played a crucial role in the establishment of the OAU. After the February, 1966, coup in Ghana, he was imprisoned in Ussher Fort, Accra, for nine months, after which he was released by the Ankrah regime through the good offices of Kenyatta. He came to Kenya in 1966 and served as an adviser in the Ministry of Tourism, becoming a Kenyan citizen in 1969. In Kenya, Makonnen established what he had conceived to be an African cultural holiday village in Mombasa (at *Shimo la Tewa*) and continued to be a generous friend and father to African freedom fighters, African Americans and West Indians. Particularly noticeable, in my view, has been the succour and comfort he provided to South African refugees in Nairobi. In this respect, I would want to remember Sefako Mukoka and most importantly Jessica Okondo. Jessica was one of the closest people to Makonnen in his late years.

In his final years, Makonnen became increasingly perturbed with the general results of independence. African unity remained elusive. Too often, he felt excessive materialism, pomp and circumstance, had become overriding preoccupations of independent Africa.

Makonnen is one of the last of his generation to pass away and the younger generation would do well to learn from his ideals, dedication and struggle.

Freedom Lives

Draft of the; Call for the Seventh Pan-African Congress.

It is almost a century since the Pan-Africanist Movement first stirred the hearts and minds of its intellectual midwives. Henry Sylvester Williams, W.E.B. Du Bois, Henry Brown, and Bishop Walters crystallized through the foundation of this movement, a seed which has gone on to grow into a tree rooted firmly in the collective aspirations of people of African descent, to see the emancipation of the African people of the world and their unity, as a national destiny of our people.

The birth of the concept, emerged at the hightide of imperialism when the western colonial powers were fresh from the conference tables, on which Africa was carved up and apportioned amongst them. The subjugation and bondage of the African, at home and in the diaspora had reached a new stage, slavery had conceded defeat to free trade requiring "the pacification" of natives for purposes of the colonial trade.

In the, *Address to the Nations of the World* by the Pan-African Conference of 1900 (London), with foresight, the founding fathers saw the problem of the twentieth century as "the problem of the colour line". Furthermore, they appealed to the nations of the world to "respect the integrity and independence of the first Negro States of Abyssinia, Liberia, Haiti, and the rest, and let the inhabitants of these States, the independent tribes of Africa, the Negroes of the West Indies and America, and the black subjects of all nations take courage, strive ceaselessly, and fight bravely, that they may prove to the world their incontestable right to be counted among the great brotherhood of mankind". This sentiment was echoed in poetry by Pixley Isaka Seme, that Africa, "waking with that morning gleam, shine as thy sister lands with equal beam".

The Pan-Africanist Movement has a proven track record. It has punctuated the history of the 20th century with its Congresses which

24

have served as summary and conceptually decisive points in the history of African emancipation in general and anti-colonialism in particular. The 1945 Congress was an important turning point, in as far as, it from then on translated ideas into practice on the African continent, with the successes and failures of the independence movement as we have come to know it. Crucial in this exercise of translation were minds like Padmore, Nkrumah, Makonnen, Kenyatta, Koinange and Abrahams. The message of Nkrumah at the onset of Ghanaian independence was that "the independence of Ghana is meaningless unless it is linked to the total liberation of Africa".

Since the close of the colonial era, the final chapter of which African enfranchisement in South Africa, in a de-racialized or post-Apartheid South Africa is becoming the starting point, we have seen unfold before our eyes, a wrap-up of colonialism. But indeed, as the wind of change swept southwards across the continent, over the last quarter century, neocolonialism became entrenched as a definition and reality of post-colonialism.

It was Nyerere, who in his *Dilemma of the Pan-Africanist* asked that "the question we now have to answer is whether Africa shall maintain this internal separation as we defeat colonialism, or whether our earlier proud boast...I am an African... shall become a reality". The cry for the "second independence" among the masses of the African people, was first heard during the rising following the murder of Patrice Lumumba in the Congo. Grinding and abject poverty, disease, endemic famine in large areas, with little hope of amelioration, has become the condition of humanity in Africa. As the twentieth century races to a close, we live in societies which too often show little regard for life and rights. Are we progressing or retrogressing?, some people ask. The elites of African society remain the mimic men decried so eloquently early this century by Casely-Hayford, Attoh-Ahuma, and Sekyi. Fanon saw little good in them, indeed many have come to agree that they intellectually will "come to pass" before the real builders of a united and therefore developmentally viable Africa, accomplish that mission. It is worth remembering that no single African nationalist leader has denied the relevance of African unity as the destination of African nationalism.

The Seventh Congress would have to address the place of the diaspora among Africans. The rights of the diaspora in Africa, today and tomorrow, need to be clarified.

Today, over half of Africa is engulfed in wars of differing intensities. The world has geopolitically become a unipolar world dominated by the United States. The IMF and the World Bank supervise an economic order which rather than providing means for African development and growth structurally adjusts Africa into increasing poverty and hardship. We need to develop new strategies and rededicate ourselves to the struggle for African emancipation both on the continent and in the diaspora. We call on all African patriots to heed the lament of the crying masses; crying for hope, bread, justice and emancipation. We are calling for participation in the Seventh Pan-Africanist Congress.

A century is a particularly measured historical benchmark for the assessment of the distance we have put behind us, in the quest for our ideals, and more importantly the rendering of accounts, for what we have achieved or failed to achieve, in the interim. How far down freedomways? How far still to go? Which direction do we take? Who are we? Who are "we these people", who Martin Luther King promised "will see the promised land"? How vindicated is Garvey's testimony of an "awakened Africa that shall never go back to sleep". It is a time to do a calculation of the profit and loss of the Pan-African project; render the balance sheet of the attempt by Africans to roll back centuries of oppression, lay down the burden of those interests which have for so long held us in subordination.

Our salvation lies in our own hands. We are the architects of our own freedom. This is a truth which stares us resolutely in the face. It is a point we need to remind ourselves of. Let us come together to discuss and resolve the burning issues of African freedom. We owe this to ourselves and the generations after us.

From a Debating Platform to a Transformatory Organization - What We Demand of African Governments

Submission to the Preparatory Meeting of the 7th Pan-African Congress, Kampala, Uganda. 9th September 1993.

Introduction.

We are saying that, we should organize and not agonize, organize and resist more, than weep and lament. It is cheery language and spritely expression, which serves to rally primeval instincts, the call of the roots. There are many who will say that all this is more easily said than done, that the history of the African peoples' struggle at the mass levels of social life, has been more an exposition of a litany of woe, than an attempt to grapple with the premises of domination and rule in colonial and post-colonial Africa; to pursue freedom as a practical and fairly immediately realizable endeavour, than an endless analysis of suffering, for clearly utopian ideals.

This argument is particularly suggestive, on account of the fact that, Africa today is going through an extremely ugly, recessive and destructive period, in which economic, cultural, and social differences are becoming areas of open contention, sharp conflict and contradiction, often seeking solutions through violent methods and exceptional routinal means. The post-colonial experience in Africa offers us precious little to be loudly proud about. We appear to be caught up in a "mission impossible" in as far as overall social, cultural, political and economic progress are concerned.

I am of the view that, this developmental *cul de sac*, arises out of the fact that the post-colonial state throughout Africa indeed has been in all instances, to different degrees neo-colonial solutions. The socio-structural linkages to the apron strings of the metropolitan powers of the world established under colonial rule remain largely unrevised and inherited. African independence, as we have come to understand it in

27

the second half of this century is ultimately premised on the acceptance of the partition of Africa, thrust on us, a little over a century ago. Did we not exist before these demarcations and identities were foisted on us?

Meaningful freedom will emerge only with the total negation of the impositions of 1885, their subsequent protocols, and their more profound and fundamental implications for African people both on the continent and in the diaspora. We can however not simply wish away the current borders. Rather, we must with the help of all positively interested parties forge cross-border linkages in all spheres of activity on the continent. African governments are slowly realizing that, African states created and handed down by retreating colonial powers have proven to be unviable economic, political and cultural entities. Unity is our only solution if we mean to march in step with the rest of humankind towards greater emancipation and progress.

What African Governments can do for African Unity

As the African masses find voice for democracy and popular political expression, hope and expectations of the betterment of the human condition is again beginning to resurface in the social consciousness of African people. It is still early days, to forecast the destination of the contemporary climate for democratic changes in the organization of African societies. But whatever the short or long term fate of the contemporary democratic challenge becomes, the unity of African people is a prerequisite for whichever paradigm for progress we envisage.

We would need to go forward from the 7th Pan-African Congress with a mandate and programme for the establishment of a movement with social, political, cultural and economic components, which will champion and articulate the aspirations for unity in Africa. African governments should be encouraged to tolerate or even assist the proliferation of this movement. This may not in all instances be easy, especially where such a movement is construed as challenge for the attention of the African masses. However, if we start from those societies which have already installed open political cultures, slowly progress will be made.

I am suggesting that a discussion of this and attendant issues be placed on the agenda. It will be a step in the direction of organizing and not agonizing.

The Cause of Our Times - Pan-Africanism Revisited

16th November 1989
Nairobi

Dear Comrade

Greetings. I hope this letter finds you in good health. I should have written earlier but a fairly hectic itinerary of meetings in and out of Kenya has stalled my reply to you. Further complicating the situation is the fact that, I have never been a consistent letter-writer. Letter writing has never come easily to me. I don't have any problems with formal letters, but letters which require the expression of personal feelings or emotions I have difficulty with, especially the psychologically "bare-all" type of letter. I am not suggesting that I do not exhibit emotions. I do enough of this and sometimes indeed too much of it. My problem is that when I write a letter which forces me to confront my feelings and emotions *post ipso facto*, and relate them to another person, it all becomes extractively tortuous. I have no problem with keeping a personal diary. The truth and reality of what I write in there is it least for now between myself and my diary. It has not been shared with any human. Enough of my apologetics about writing a reply to your letter. I have now been able to get it off my desk. Never mind the light years it has taken.

The deepening crisis of African society intimidates hope, and condemns our immediate vision to a landscape of misery and desperation. Africa seems to enjoy inflicting wounds on itself. A history of famine, mass involuntary translocation, epidemics, and endless and proliferating wars have put the era of early independence into the depths of our experience. It is a bygone age and if you like an almost idyllic era only recalled with nostalgia. We live in an Africa in retardation, an Africa which appears to have lost it's way towards emancipation and development. What we know is that we will get there, what appears also to be the case is that, the period of directionlessness and sorrow is not going to end by some unpredictable stroke of fortune. At the time of independence we did not expect immediate paradise on earth, but there was an infectious hope that progress and development was within grasp of the emergent generation of African youth.

The Sudan was at war literally before independence in 1956. In August 1955, the Torit Mutiny had announced historically the beginnings of a war which has since then, ebbed and flowed to the present day. Tension and conflict in Mauritania today bears uncanny comparisons with the Sudan. Till today, slavery exists in the Afro-Arab borderlands in countries like the Sudan and Mauritania. Liberia and Sierra Leone have in recent years been overtaken by an increasingly festering war. The days of war in Uganda do not appear to be over. Eritrea has been the child of much pain and suffering. Mozambique is on its knees on account of a war the reason for which both sides cannot offer palpable explanations. Chad has been at war for most of its post-independence period. Angola has never seen any peace since the period of the anti-colonial war. Niger and Mali are faced with armed internal conflict. The harrowing face of the Nigerian civil war, and famine-ravaged Ethiopia's journey through an era of fratricidal conflict, the spasmodic outbursts of bloodletting in Rwanda and Burundi, plus numerous smaller conflicts in Northern Ghana, Cabinda, Togo, Djibouti, Congo Brazzaville, Casamance in the Senegal, Gambia, the Cameroons/Nigeria southern border region, the Zambia/Zaire border region and elsewhere on the African continent has painted to humanity at large an image of a people, lost in unending agony and unable to help themselves. Somalia is caught up in a fratricidal war which beats reason. The Congo/Zaire was propelled into independence in chaos, international intrigue, conspiracy, and the assassination of its first president Lumumba. We have seen tragic and bizarre tyrannies in Marcias Nguema's Equatorial Guinea, Amin's Uganda, Bokassa's Central African Empire. Even countries, which have shown over the years relative peace, like Gabon, Malawi and Swaziland have in the recent past developed turbulent political cultures with some measure of blood-letting. Kenya is doggedly tormenting itself. It is all a sorry tale. Cases of durable peace and political sanity like Tanzania and Botswana are exceptional.

Thank you very much for your paper entitled *A Call for Revolutionary Pan-Africanism*. It is an exciting paper and definitely contributes to the emerging debate on the Pan-Africanist cause in theory, and what is to be done in practice. I am also happy to note that as you say in your letter you recently came across a copy of my letter addressed to B.F. Bankie of the 31st March, 1989, drawing attention to the plans to convene the 7th Pan-African Congress. I am afraid for the time being, we appear to have run into some difficulty with regards to the convention of this meeting, due to philosophically contrasting contentions, organisational problems and financial implications. I am however, not unduly worried because I believe in due course of time, these difficulties will be resolved. Furthermore, I am convinced that we need some time to iron out some fundamental issues attendant on the impending 7th Pan-African Congress. The Congress should have a democratic basis for its convention. Are we going to represent ourselves? Can African states in the light of experience be entrusted with advancing actively, a serious Pan-African programme, or should the leadership of this be essentially the domain of civil society? Who is going to be given a voice? On what basis is this selection going to be done? Who is entitled to call this Congress or any other subsequent Congress? On the basis of whose mandate is this going to be done? Can anybody call a Congress and describe it as "a legitimate" Pan-African Congress? How do we protect the Congress from falling into the hands of people, groups or forces with doubtful or questionable intentions?

We would need to resolve a whole range of conceptual, tactical and strategic issues, in order for the Congress to have true significance for the future. To rush headlong into the Congress without the resolution of preparatory issues would render the exercise futile and empty. I am sure history would not reflect kindly on that. We would need to digest comprehensively the lessons of the past, take stock and offer viable answers for the future.

There are those who simply want to see and have their names

associated with the Congress for the limelight and the supposed "glory" that they believe this offers. There would be many, who throughout their lives have never done anything Pan-African, who would jump on the bandwagon for the Congress at the eleventh hour in order to have their names registered in history books. If they contribute tangibly to the development of our collective understanding of the issues at stake, and offer solutions to our needed organizational provisions that would be excellent. It will be a blessing in disguise. I however fear that, too many of such types are actually full-blooded opportunists who have little substantial to add to our understanding of the issues. I really hope also that it does not become another of the usual gathering of academics, that we do not make the whole matter an academic debate for scholarly windbags. The other unwelcome extreme would be the convention of a Congress, which turns out to be a Jamboree, with nebulous discussions and platitudinous statements by African government representatives each vying for a little bit of the show.

I am informed that you were at the meeting in Harare where my observations on "Who is an African" were subject to discussion. Pandi Mutoma had I believe done the groundwork for this meeting. In my view, that question is one of the crucial issues to be resolved, or rather laid to rest, before the Congress. It is one of the most immediate issues facing our "congregation". It is difficult to conceive of a Pan-African Congress for the unity and nationhood of Africans, I emphasise nationhood of Africans, if the participants are not agreed on who is an African; who belongs to the African nation; who should participate. While the question is frightfully relevant to the discussion of African unity, it is at the same time, an issue or question many find too sensitive for discussion. It is often casually brushed aside and hoped that it would disappear. But its centrality to the whole issue of African unity cannot be wished away or avoided. It needs to be addressed with the seriousness and urgency that it deserves. It needs to be treated with frankness and forthrightness.

In too many parts of Africa, people who do not regard themselves as Africans are regarded as such by Africans. Being African is virtually equated with citizenship. I think this is often deliberate and wicked. As I have often insisted, if everybody is an African, then nobody is an African. I am not suggesting anything chauvinistic. I have never been an inward-looking essentially xenophobic mind, and do not at present intend to become that. I am only too aware of the equality and commonality of humankind. Needless to say, we have this century been witness to too much evil and crimes against humanity by xenophobic minds, and fascist social systems, to entertain in all sanity such warped ideas. But history demands of us that, we stand up and be counted, that we define for ourselves clearly on the basis of African history and culture, as a strand in the history of humankind, what in our experience and collective being define us in historical and cultural distinction to the rest of humankind. Our contribution to human history, and the making of the culture of homo sapiens today and yesterday. What makes us Africans.

All the principal historico-cultural groupings on this planet are aware and respect their heritage. None of the peoples colonized by Europe have heathenised their traditional religious lore. They have invariably at the worst placed such traditional practices on par with the received religions. In several instances, such imported religious practices have been adequately indigenized. Without the recognition and usage of our historical and cultural baggage, we are no people. All peoples in the world develop and advance on the basis of their culture and history, while absorbing whatever can be absorbed from outside which improves what they already have, without abandoning their own. We cannot earn self-respect and equality in the eyes of other peoples on this planet if we demonstrate ourselves to be people without any historical or cultural belongings they are proud of, or will to keep. We cannot develop, if we treat ourselves as people who have no respect for their own, but respect for the cultural belongings of others. The Europeans, keenly aware of their culture and history today are striving towards unity, the Chinese have a strong sense of identity which goes beyond the borders of mainland China the heartland of the Celestial Kingdom, the Arabs are rightfully aware of their nationhood, the Hindus share a historical and rich culture. Jews are scattered all over the world, but are united by history and culture. Who is an African? Without an answer to that, we cannot discuss unity in practice, for we would not even know who to unite with, on what basis, and for what concrete historical objectives. It is because we have not resolved this issue that we still are taught and fed on other people's view or interpretation of African history. Because we do not know who we are, we are unable to conceive our history and culture "from inside". This is why African history as it is still generally taught, is more the history of the westerner in Africa, than the history of the African in Africa i.e. with the African at the centre of his or her own history. The African is marginalized in the rendition of his/her own history.

At this stage I believe we need to draw as many minds as possible into the discussion, and enrich our understanding of the core issues at stake. We can make use of the present period for this purpose. This is why I think your discussion paper is particularly useful. It concretely supports this process.

I have a number of observations to make regarding the emerging debate. I hope my views will be seen as a contribution to the debate. You may recall that some time ago, when we met at Duduville, Nairobi, for the conference on *Constitutionalism in Eastern and Southern Africa* organized by (The Organization for Social Science Research in Eastern and Southern Africa) OSSREA, I did indicate to you and Yash Tandon over breakfast at the Utalii Hotel, that I am convinced beyond any shadow of a doubt, that the missing link at the present conjuncture in African history in the struggle for African emancipation, democracy and development, based on the principles of self-determination and anti-imperialism, is the Pan-Africanist link. It is that link, which would define the structural framework for the historical negation of the Berlin Conference's carve-up of Africa a century ago. Philistines and *etatists* among us will say, "but hey! you have the (Organization of African Unity) OAU, you have (Economic Community of West African States) ECOWAS, you have the (Preferential Trade Area) PTA, (Southern African Development Coordinating Conference) SADCC, what more Pan-Africanist do you want"? For such people, Pan-Africanism is simply the geographical or regional aggregation of neocolonial Africa. Would you believe it, I have even come across people talking of regional or sub-regional

Pan-Africanism. For them Pan-Africanism remains simply a reaction to colonialism. This position leads directly into "continentalism", that is, the argument that Pan-Africanism means still for us today, the unity of the African continent in the first place, a unity of post-colonial states, and not as I would say the unity of peoples, whose history and culture derive from the African continent, and are conscious of this affinity and wish to develop these roots as a basis for the social and economic emancipation of African people. You see, my definition fundamentally recognizes the link with the diaspora as more important than, the notion of continental unity per se, which is essentially geographical. In other words, the unity of the greater part of this continent, logically would emerge more as a consequence than a cause. Again in other words, if people of African history and descent unite, that is the African nation unites, most of the continent of Africa will unite.

These days, the philistines of this world want to make some of us feel that, to work for and aspire towards Pan-African ideals is obscene; that Pan-African ideals died with Du Bois, Nkrumah, Toure, Keita, Kenyatta among others, and the OAU's foundation. Of course this is poppycock. Our worst enemies in the quest for our Pan-Africanist destiny on this continent today are those interest groups tied firmly to the maintenance of the mosaic of states which make up Africa today. Before I forget, let me point out that, what we have on the African continent today are states, neocolonial states, and not nation-states as the apologists of neocolonialism often say.

The racial definition of an African is flawed. It is unscientific and hence untenable. No serious mind today would use the race concept in any way except as an instrument for poetic imagery. What I am saying is that no group of people has been "pure" from time immemorial. Notions of purity belong to the language of fascists and the rubbish-bin of science. But before my observations are misunderstood let me take the argument into another direction. Most Africans are black, but not all Africans are black, and not all blacks have African cultural and historical roots. Jews range from blond to black. Another example, Arabs also do. I am not denying the fact that this continent is the cradle of the African and as far as we know today the birthplace of homo sapiens. There are many groups in Africa today which are not African, do not describe themselves as African or wish to be so regarded, peoples whose cultures and histories are linked and derived from extra-African sources. Needless to say, they are full citizens and must always remain full and equal citizens in all respects to the Africans amongst whom they live, and I dare say apartheid and caste systems of any kind should not be tolerated, since we seek ultimately the freedom of all humanity, and the untrammelled social intercourse of all the peoples of this earth.

The cultures of these minorities who live amongst us have helped in the enrichment and cosmopolitanization of social life and tastes in large areas of Africa. Some of these groups may in due course of time and history come to regard themselves as African. All peoples have a right to their culture and its usage. But cultures are not stagnant or fixed entities. Cultural change is a permanent feature of all societies. No human group has from time immemorial been hermetically sealed, culturally or otherwise. Diffusion, interpenetration and mixing is the real substance of the historical process, but at every given historical conjuncture, people are formed by the existent culture they produce and reproduce. But cultures are created and also wither. When cultures die, the people whose culture declines and falls, do not necessarily physically die, they become other people. Often they are absorbed by more dominant cultures.

Obviously, there is constantly a world culture in creation. This universal cultural fund is shared literally by all people. The phenomenology of a global village underscores this point. It is a cultural fund to which we all in principle contribute, but in practice, it is the dominant or hegemonic cultures of the world, which determine active cultural development in this sphere. There are many, particularly among westerners who too easily and rather ethnocentrically, equate universal culture with western culture. In a world of competing cultures, growth, prosperity and cultural advancement is a factor of economic and political power. This is why, for example in the case of South Africa, under Afrikaner National Party rule, the language of the Afrikaner, Afrikaans which had started as a patois was developed and rapidly elevated to a language of modern science and technology, and forced on to the rest of the population.

Culture, history, attachment to these and consciousness of identity, and not skin colour, primarily defines the African. The fact that most Africans or people of African historical and cultural descent are black is only one characteristic, a bonus which generalizes and typifies Africans. And indeed, I dare say, for us, in the absence of a strong unifying religion or single language, colour has become an easy and fortunate identifying attribute of most people who regard themselves as African. Thus while others have used our colour to distinguish us for oppression and denigration, it is at the same time one of the most fortunate coincidences which identifies a people whose cultures have over centuries been woefully shattered by their oppressors. While in recent centuries slavery by Europe and the Arab world has hung heavily on African history, Africans have existed long before these periods, and cannot be defined as a people mainly on the basis of this experience. Definitionally, being African is not simply or essentially a reaction to the history of oppression. It includes this, but also stands before and transcends this history.

Major features of the nations of humankind, include commonality of religion, geography, language, and mythology. But in no instance are all these features present, or present to the same extent, and as I read somewhere many years ago in a source I can now not remember, "no one can say that when the register of nations was being drawn up nation a, or b, was not on the list".

The framework of the state in Africa derives historically from the inheritance of the protocols of the Berlin Conference and its aftermath. This has largely determined the restricted expression of nationalist parties within former colonial borders. Our national consciousness as Africans, or rather, what is generally understood as African Nationalism, is in an important and not insignificant sense defined by the historical parameters and the political framework bequeathed by Berlin, 1885. The terms people used since the beginnings of the struggle for colonial freedom have been Kenyan nationalism Somali nationalism, Nigerian nationalism and so on. In other words, African nationalism has hitherto been seen largely as a product or response to specific colonial powers and administration. It is thus seen, as I earlier suggested, as part of western history in Africa. These days some observers are pressing into argument terms like, Zulu nationalism, Ashanti nationalism, Ewe nationalism, Ibo nationalism or Baganda nationalism; phenomena which in the past were often referred to as tribalism during the early post-colonial period.

Nationalism in Africa has been actualized only through the colonial or neo-colonial state. The basis of national expression by African people in the era of the third decade of post-colonialism in Africa has fostered a patriotic symbolism created by structures put into place by European imperialists at the beginning of the colonial encounter. Under the leadership of the westernized elite, these identities are starting to enjoy mythologism amongst Africans. Identities left in place by the departing colonial powers are glorified and sanctimoniously revered. The ruling classes in Africa are as a basis for their legitimacy, investing these identities with notions of "volksgeist". When are we going to be happy with being simply first and foremost emphatically Africans and then, Yoruba, Nguni, Sotho-Tswana, Fula, before Ugandan, Kenyan, Sudanese or Namibian. Such approaches will give us back our historical and cultural belongings.

Recognition of the vitality of ethnic identities does not in itself constitute "tribalism", or excessive inward-lookingness. Ethnic identities provide local varieties of African culture. The cultural unity of Africa is built into the fact that, such local varieties of culture are essentially variations on fairly related and similar themes. It is only when such identities become instruments of chauvinism and the apportionment of resources, or become criteria for access to resources in the multi-ethnic states which African countries today are, that "tribalism" occurs. Thus tribalism is atavistic and retrogressive, given the realities of the contemporary world. Organic political and economic unity of Africans is the only arguably viable way to reduce the significance or petty divisiveness of ethnicities in Africa. In a united structure with many nationalities/ethnicities sharing a common umbrella nationhood, no ethnicity/nationality can enjoy structural preeminence.

I am also not saying that, contemporary African states are not fundamental realities in our collective existence today. Far from that, indeed we would need to learn to bend and use these structures for the achievement of our higher ideals of unity and common identity. What the post-colonial experience has demonstrated is that, none of these states we have is economically or politically viable. The present African flags are only institutional representations of imperial devolution of partial political power. They are indeed, derivations of the agreements between western powers about Africa in a way inspired as far back as a hundred odd years ago. What have we called ourselves or people like ourselves throughout the millennia of African history? Are we still prepared to carry on as simply products of the westerner, bondsmen of our old imperial overlords? It is an impossible basis to develop. Every day that this charade continues we postpone our freedom.

I am not suggesting that simply changing our state identities, so-called national identities of the neocolonial world, will automatically mean freedom. The problem is socio-structural in a global sense. It is embedded in the global political economy and the culture it supports. We are indeed products of this, but we are at the same time dialectically the only real agency of its eventual negation.

My thinking suggests that the solution of the national and agrarian questions, in pursuit of the democratic ideal and the emancipation principle in Africa, can be achieved only through the Pan-African framework, in theory and practice. This framework provides a reference point which transcends western colonialism, and reaches into the depths of African culture and history. This is where the definition of Africa's contribution to human history can be ultimately understood. This is where we must hinge our rudder.

The three decades of African independence have in substance meant the rise of small-producers, small-holders, petty traders, soldiery, clerks, bureaucrats and socio-economically similar groups which have in the overall political economy of the late 20th century world served largely as local elements functioning in a system created and dominated by external metropolitan interests. These groups have demonstrated a poor acumen for capital accumulation, which has been matched in inverse proportion to a consumption style fired by the reference images of western consumption patterns. They have run the state in Africa essentially in support of structures put in place under colonialism and inherited with little alteration since the onset of the independence era. They have thus guaranteed a neo-colonial solution to African development in favour of the former colonial masters in economics, politics, culture, education and ideology in general. They have served largely as inferior surrogates and trojan horses for big power interests. They have historically largely turned their backs on their traditional roots in favour often of uncritical and intellectually unsavoury westernism.

Thirty to forty years ago, when Fanon was heaping vituperation on this class of emergent Africans, few could have imagined how this element would grow and reproduce itself and its culture quite overindulgently. How it could come to believe its own lies so steadfastly. How it can live and expand in increasing economic stagnation and retrogression, ordered by tyrannical political and military state machines, while continuously making believe that the solutions to African development can be found through western agency, or the hack philosophies and concepts spawned by eurocentric intellectual fashion-conscious thinkers.

The post-second world war Bretton Woods Agreement and its subsequent institutions like the IMF and the World Bank, have been deployed to serve the preservation of western economic hegemony over wider global interests. This principle is built into the operations of the General Agreement on Tariffs and Trade. The relationship between the ACP countries and the European Community is another institutional case in point. I am of course not suggesting that, in one fell swoop we can negate and disengage from the global economic periphery. That must remain a strategic objective. But our tactics must remain very flexible; working towards unity, emancipation and societal development.

In order to maintain neo-colonialism, metropolitan interests have quietly supported their local allies in the maintenance of cultures of repression in Africa, where until fairly recently dictatorial single-party states or military regimes drew heavily on public means to maintain tin-pot dictatorships which have perfected the art of the brutalization

41

of the citizenry. Recent changes in Eastern Europe, and the ascendancy of the US as supremo, or political boss among the big powers has created a climate in which the structures of political pluralism under capitalism, have become the new credo for the organization of social order. Meanwhile the tin gods of African politics remain largely unwilling to give ground except under considerable pressure. The tyrannies in many cases continue. The mass of the populace remains cowed and poorer by the day, a citizenry benumbed, deafened and silenced. Intimidation, intolerance and scant concern for civil and group rights remains the order of the day. The masses have for too long been muzzled, while the ruling and influential groups continue to indulge in excesses of pillage and plunder of the public resource, under conditions in many cases, as I have earlier indicated, of state-sponsored terror. The dictatorships which emerged soon after the beginning of the independence era are slowly yielding to pressures for democracy. Since 1990 several decrepit regimes and old dictators have been chased out of power. Others will follow.

The quality of life in all senses of the term for the African people has been over the past two decades in steady decline. The IMF and World Bank policies are in practice meant to reinforce the dependence of Africa on so-called donor support, the imputed largesse of the western powers, but which in fact increases Africa's dependency, and ties us further to the apron strings of the metropolitan powers. Africa's "debt" enriches imperialism. The trick has been to structurally undervalue our exports through devaluation whilst they increase the prices of their imports to us. They decide what prices should be put on our exports, and also what prices should be put on our imports. Imperialism has no intention of allowing us the economic and technological wherewithal to develop because they know too well that, that might imply a global shift in the centre of wealth and technological power.

In a statement made recently (1989) by Conable, the Head of the World Bank, he suggests that the standard of living of the African today is what is was thirty years ago. True enough. I find it in a way a shameful admission from the mouth of someone, who is top dog for one of the most important institutions responsible and controlling the fate of this condition. He is right though, when he says that, African bureaucracies are bloated beyond efficiency and good economic sense. These bureaucracies have no positive relevance for the developmental needs of Africa. They are parasitic structures preying on the diminishing returns of the productive sectors of society.

I would add that Africa's development to my mind is inconceivable without unity, for without unity we would forever be pawns in the game of the metropolitan powers dividing us, creating unnecessary rivalries and supporting surrogates who can never stand on their own feet. Writing off "debts", is a way of avoiding any fundamental and critical examination of the system which makes the toilers of the earth, on whom the extraction of the fat of the land is burdened, remain ever trapped in "debt"; economically enslaved and preserving the fundamental structure of servitude which has for centuries, alas, too long held them in fee. By releasing the built-up pressure in the system in the form of debt-relief, the system does not explode. The metropolitan powers are suggesting that only their kindness and christian magnanimity is saving Africa. It is "the whiteman's burden" all over again. The system is in order, by implication. The South is not working hard enough. We are a lazy lot, they suggest. The North is working steadily harder, constantly working better than the wretched of the earth. The South is producing less all the time. It is a curious logic used to justify the rapacity of the system.

The metropolitan powers seize the moral high-ground, sermonizing and pontificating to the rest of us, on human rights, democracy, etc; indeed slave masters ministering to the moral, political, and economic needs of the slaves. Has the South African apartheid system of our contemporary world not been more vicious and dehumanizing than the much vilified Soviet-sponsored socialism of Eastern Europe? The western world has been more than willing to do anything, to bring to a rapid end this shabby version of institutionalised socialism in the name of freedom. Why has the western world at the state level apart from its half-hearted support of sanctions, been hardly willing to provide the support and pressure necessary to bring to an end the apartheid system, which has been matched in its evil, only by the

43

Hitlerite idea? Most of the telling pressure for change in South Africa in the west was structured within civil society in general and non-conservative groups in particular. Politically conservative western society has tended to symphatize with the rulers of the apartheid system, at heart, they have always been inclined to regard the African as a lesser human. Take for example the British wartime leader Winston Churchill as recorded by C.L. Sulzberger in a recollection of the 10th of July, 1956.

> Following are some other topics Churchill discussed. America should be temperate and wise about taking time to solve its Negro problem. "After all, you can't take twenty million of them into your belly just like that. Nonsense to say that the black is the same as the white". He called for a copy of this morning's *Daily Sketch* with a picture of a Negro Salvation Army singer followed by a white Salvation Army lass. "Is that what they are going to have in Heaven?" he asked. "Is that what I am going to find there? If so, it is no place for me. I don't intend to go to a place like that. ...The Commonwealth will get worse, not better. No point taking in all these Blacks like the Gold Coast. They will go their own way. And in another generation the Indians will be even more Indian (1).

The simple truth is that, many western conservatives have been socio-structural bedfellows of racists, who see the African as a lesser phenomenon than the western man in Europe or elsewhere. When apartheid is finally legally dismantled, it is very likely to be done in such a way that the economic and social benefits of the system as they have over the decades accrued to the whites remains largely intact. The loot must remain with the historical looters. A small group of African elite will emerge politically centre-stage and spotlighted as government, but as very junior partners within the power-elite. It will be a South African version of the post-colonial elite we have seen emerge in Africa, since the onset of the independence era some thirty years ago. It is the final instalment to the creation of the post-colonial elite this side of this century, and at the close of this millennium. What is being achieved in South Africa today is progress, but it is hardly the end of the road.

In Namibia where I lived from August 1990 till the beginning of 1992, there are areas in choice neighbourhoods like Ludwigsdorf, Klein Windhoek, Olympia and Luxury Hill, where as and when you drive or walk through with your black face, the whites who overwhelmingly dominate in these areas look at you in amazement and surprise, like, "what are you doing here?". "You don't belong". Now, the irony of the situation is that, here you are an African, with as black a face as you can ever imagine, in the middle of Africa, where people with your physionogmy have generally lived from time immemorial, at the close of the 20th century you are regarded by white settlers and their descendants as a strange species in their midst. It is simply not funny. It is curiously understandable, but roundly absurd. Well, you may say Namibia is only recently free from colonial rule and has for so long suffered under the apartheid system. I say wait a minute! I have seen the same sort of thing in Nairobi, in areas like Muthaiga, parts of Karen, etc.

In 1980, during my lecture tour in China, I remember my hosts took me to a park at the end of the old western commercial quarter of Shanghai called the *Bund*, they informed me that before China "stood up" there was a sign in the park reading, "dogs and Chinese not allowed". For the Chinese, it is now history they ridicule. *Slegs Blankes* signs are no longer to be seen in public places in South Africa but poverty and deprivation will for some time to come maintain its implications in the social life of people. Africa is the only part of the world where this sort of phenomenon is on this scale today; where the natives in their masses (with the exception of only a small portion of natives belonging to the elite) in the last decade of the 20th century are largely flunkeys and servants of settlers from all corners of the world. I have been to restaurants in Kenya, Zimbabwe, Namibia where the only Africans you see are the waiters and other servants. Such phenomena are I think unpleasant and painful for any sensible African. Those Africans who accept such phenomenology, without notice or pain, are essentially people who have accepted inferior status, and have internalised it to a point that they no longer even realise that, their whole existential structure is premised on inequality to the westerner and her/his culture.

Following from what I have just argued, another important point to be remembered is that development is impossible, if it is not premised on our own historico-cultural conditions. No society in the history of mankind has ever been able to progress socially and economically, on the basis of an unrestrictedly borrowed culture or cultures. We seem to have a penchant of unquenchable proportions for imitating and borrowing indiscriminately. Nothing of our own ever appears good enough for our purposes. In this respect, our imitative habits are as if, we labour under the impression that mimicry and imitation would transform our under-developed condition into a developed one. The externals of the westerner have become our image of the desirable. The leading groups in African society are the main culprits for this condition. Writing in 1911, Attoh Ahuma in his own superb brand of flowery eloquence of vintage quality, had this to say about, *The Whiteman and his West African Understudy*. I give him the length he deserves on this issue:

> Imitation, it is said, is the sincerest form of flattery; but according to Jonathan Swift in his Cadenus and Vanesa, "flattery is the food of fools". Histrionism is undoubtedly the special forte of the educated West African; he is a copyist to the pitch of profane excellence. The Whiteman has his vices as well as his virtues, and sometimes the vices of his virtues. To follow him half-way therefore, is not, and cannot be the sincerest form of flattery. The average West African of the Molluscan Order, is a clever imitator of everything the whiteman thinks, and does, and says, particularly in the outward appearance and observance. If he doffed his coat and went about in his shirt sleeves in broad daylight, by reason of our intolerable tropical heat, his Native understudy faithfully followed suit; if, in the cool of the evening, he discarded his headgear, the backboneless myrmidons did likewise. As he lands in the latest things in vogue, his echo takes full notes, and in less than seven weeks, like a puppet or marionette he sports the identical style and fashion. Thanks to the letters C.O.D., facilities are afforded the young upstart to gratify his unworthy ambition. What the Whiteman eats, he eats; what

46

he drinks and smokes, he drinks and smokes, thereby securing what, in his deluded opinion, is the hallmark of respectability, civilization and refinement. If his lord and master holds a cigar in a peculiar manner, it is copied; his gait, mode of expression, his expletives, smiles, laughter and other mannerisms and peculiarities, are all taken in wholesale, and reproduced with the fidelity of an Edisonian Phonograph. These are the things the black wretch in his Boeotian ignorance and folly, regards as signs of perfect manhood, this thin veneer of polish, and there the lesson ends.(2)

As I have elsewhere said, the African elite consumes what it does not produce, and supervises the production of what we do not consume (3). In the thirty lean years of independence, it has shown no real determination to change this condition. A generation ago, or at least, when our sense of who we are started dawning seriously on some of us of the present generation, we hoped that the desire to make black Europeans of us in Africa, would come to the definite end it deserved. The previous generation of westernized Africans had become submissively infatuated and idiotically enthralled with western culture. If one spoke with a European accent, he or she was immediately socially accepted as a superior breed. "Christian names", which in effect were simply European names were preferred. There were those, who went as far as changing their African names to make them sound European. Thus in South Africa, among the Xhosa, *Mtimkhulu* or literally "big tree" became *Grooteboom* (Dutch for the same). Among the Fanti of the Gold Coast, *Egya Obu*, literally, Mr. Obu (Mr Rock) became Rockson, *Egya Kuntu* (Mr Blanket) became Mr. Blankson. We accepted too easily western arguments about the primitiveness of our religious practices, it was all heathen, idolatry, "the work of darkness and Satan". Some Arabs still regard Africa as a "civilization vacuum".

Possibly, no other factor was as crucial in denting the African's confidence in his or her culture as the subversion of the status of the religion of his or her ancestors. Christianity and Islam were not accepted as alternatives, on the basis of equality, but as superior replacements to religious attitudes and systems which had for centuries sustained Africans. True enough, some African religious practices were and are outdated. What they need is not abandonment but reform and adaptation. Where Christianity was accepted, too often, any attempt to thoroughly Africanise it is rejected, both by clerics faithful to the metropolitan sources of the respective denominations, and also, the elite which has most thoroughly accepted cultural inferiority and the notion that, anything from the west, is better than that which is indigenous. When after the Meiji Restoration in Japan, the status and function of Shintoism superseded Buddhism in Japan, the Japanese were asserting their historical cultural roots in a way which indeed would later accelerate their propulsion into the most advanced technological society in the world a century later. The Chinese, in spite of concessionary colonialism and attendant excesses of western subjugation held on to their religious lore. One of the most important lessons of my China journey in 1980 was that, as a "conscience collective", the Chinese regard their culture and history as central to them as Chinese in a way that Africans do not treat their culture and history. The Arab never compromised on the status of Islam in the face of western dominance, indeed the culture of the teachings of the Prophet Mohammed inspired their being. The Hindoo maintained the primacy of his or her religious heritage against tremendous odds. It was the African who for various reasons accepted the inferiority and "barbarism" of the religion of his or her ancestors. The African's inferiority is not in his or her skin, but in the mind. Without respect for what the ancestors have bequeathed, we can only as Claude Mackay many years ago said with reference to Afro-America, "bend our knees to alien gods".

In an article which appeared in 1917, in Mohammed Duse's, *The Africa Times and Orient Review*, addressing himself to the topic of *The Future of Subject Peoples*, Kobina Sekyi suggested wisely that, Africans should accept "from the West only such institutions as can be adapted to, and not such as cannot but alter, their national life" (4).

We may note with satisfaction that such wisdom has in the past been fairly common among serious thinkers concerned about the issue of African nationality, and how to press home the development effort in Africa for Africans. John Williamson Kuye in 1936, quoting the British missionary Mary Kingsley to effect, reiterated that;

> The public has been taught that all African Native Institutions are bad and unless you preserve your institutions, above all your land law, you cannot, no race can, preserve your liberty (5).

Another light of the Pan-Africanist past who had clear views on this issue was Casely Hayford. As far back as the first decade of this century, he stood with two feet firmly on the ground regarding this issue. Using the Japanese as example he asserted:

> The African may turn socialist, may preach and cry for reform until the day of judgement; but the experience of mankind shows this, that reform never comes to a class or a people unless and until those concerned have worked out their own salvation. And the lesson we have yet to learn is that we cannot depart from Nature's way and hope for real success.... Knowledge, deprived of the assimilating element which makes it natural to the one taught, renders that person but a mere imitator. The Japanese, adopting and assimilating Western culture, of necessity commands the respect of Western nations, because there is something distinctly Eastern about him. He commands to begin with, the uses of his native tongue, and has a literature of his own, enriched by translations from standard authors of other lands. He respects the institutions and customs of his ancestors, and there is an intelligent past which inspires him. He does not discard his national costume, and if, now and again, he dons Western attire, he does so as a matter of convenience, much as the Scotch, across the border, puts away, when the occasion demands it, his Highland costume (6).

Shortly before he died, C.L.R. James in an interview made a point of emphasizing the fact that, the route to African emancipation in a global sense lay squarely in the hands of the African, and no one else.

It is a theme we find repeated by Makonnen, Biko, Sobukwe, or Garvey amongst others. I like quoting Kenyatta's dedication in the opening of his "Facing Mount Kenya" where he refers to "making communion with the ancestors". Nkrumah also often made the point that, "we are the architects of our own salvation".

Another point I need to make is the fact that, in my view, putting the relationship of Africans based in the continent and those in the diaspora on a proper footing is crucial to our salvation and emancipation. It is hardly an accident that, the intellectual origins of the Pan-African movement started in the diaspora. Du Bois wrote:

> The idea of one Africa uniting the thought and ideals of all native peoples of the dark continent belongs to the twentieth century, and stems naturally from the West Indies and the United States. Here various groups of Africans, quite separate in origin, became so united in experience, and so exposed to the impact of a new culture, that they began to think of Africa as one idea and one land. Thus, late in the eighteenth century, when a separate Negro Church was formed in Philadelphia, it called itself "African"; and there were various 'African' societies in many parts of the United States. I was not, however, until 1900 that a black West Indian barrister, H. Sylvester-Williams of Trinidad, practising in London, called together a "Pan-African" Conference. This meeting attracted attention, put the word "Pan-African" in the dictionaries for the first time, and had some thirty delegates, mainly from England and the West Indies, with a few coloured Americans. The Conference was welcomed by the Lord Bishop of London, and a promise was obtained from Queen Victoria through Joseph Chamberlain not to "overlook the interest and welfare of the native races" (7).

Henry Sylvester-Williams pioneered the birth of the movement, but it was Du Bois whose persistence, intellect and organizational ability, ensured the firm establishment of the tradition. Padmore reverently writes:

> Between 1919 and 1945, Dr. Du Bois was largely responsible for the organization of five international congresses and for formulating their programmes and strategy along the path of non-violent Positive

Action. For more that thirty years, Dr. Du Bois watched over the gradual growth of the Pan-African Congress with the loving affection of a father until such time as his child had found a home on African soil (8).

We would need to address the problem of overseas Africans i.e. our people in the diaspora. They would need to have rights to the African nationality on demand in much the same way the Chinese government treats overseas Chinese, if not better. It is not by accident that the leading minds of the Pan-Africanist position were born in the diaspora. It was from that vantage point of their physical estrangement from Africa which in a way provided them the circumstantial means and condition to conceive so well the idea of Pan -Africanism. Pan-Africanism does not predate them.

Our languages are suffering slow death, and somehow we fail to understand that because our languages were until in most cases only a hundred years ago preliterate, these languages represent the living form and expression of our history, culture, and collective being. If we allow these languages to die then we cease to exist as a distinct human cultural group with its own historically endowed features and characteristics, with a specific and vital contribution to make to the march of humankind.

The question of African languages is a much misunderstood issue. There are some amongst us who have mistakenly come to believe that African languages cannot modernize to become languages of science and technology. There are many who labour under the misconception that, Africa is a tower of Babel. That there are thousands of languages which are mutually largely exclusive. Hence it is impossible to find commonalities in language use, based on our indigenous languages. This notion was born out of the colonial anthropological experience in general and colonial administration in particular.

This view suggested that Africa is made up of numerous tribes, sufficiently distinct from each other to warrant a conceptualization of the ethnographic map of Africa, along lines of the myriad of cultures suggested by missionaries and anthropologists. Apart from this serving the wishes of anthropologists to "discover their own tribes", this approach also provided means for the colonial administrators to carve up Africa in the service of their policies of divide and rule. Neville Alexander and Ngugi Wa Thiongo have drawn strong attention to this question.

It is clear to me that this legacy needs to be rolled back. For example, Jur, Anuak, Shilluk, Acholi, Langi, Chopadhola, Alur, and Luo are essentially the same language, Indeed, as I have elsewhere said, a Shilluk tribesman from Kodok in the Southern Sudan transplanted as it were to South Nyanza District in Kenya would have no difficulty understanding the dialect spoken in this area. Most would not even know that they have linguistic brethren that far. I am reminded of an Ethiopian friend, an academic, who was surprised to discover in a supermarket in Nairobi, a Borana speaking a dialect similar to his dialect of Oromo. Swati in Swaziland and South Mozambique, the Nguni languages of Mozambique and South Tanzania, Kangwane in South Africa, Zulu in South Africa, Xhosa in South Africa, Ndebele in South Africa and Matabeleland in Zimbabwe are all mutually intelligible. So also are, Sotho in Lesotho, Lozi in Zambia, Tswana in Botswana, Namibia and South Africa, Pedi in the Transvaal of South Africa. The East African interlacustrine languages are for a large part mutually intelligible clusters. Curiously Soga in Uganda has similarities to Shona in Zimbabwe. One can go on clearly to demonstrate that with some scientific work and creative ingenuity, it should be possible for us to standardize a whole range of African languages, so that we have large language areas each bigger than any of the European languages within the European continent.

Some people glibly agree that some European languages even with their small sizes of users, are viable repositories for advanced scientific work and collective expression of the historical experience of their users. African languages are quietly dismissed as unsuitable for these purposes. This is why a quarter of a century after independence, African countries continue to give seniority of place to European languages in their own social intercourse. On paper, and in their constitutions African states place indigenous languages on par with colonially inherited languages, but in practice they favour the colonial languages. This practice ensures the superiority of the western man in post-colonial Africa, and cuts off the African masses, who form the overwhelming majority of the population based in the countryside, from advances in ideas, science and social organisation, from the mainstream of the march of humankind.

The elite, by accepting the role of guardians of this dispensation, by definition, place themselves squarely in the slot of supporters for the maintenance of the backwardness of African society and its appendage status, to western culture and society. It is this, and more, which has made the African elite such shabby replicas of the western man in Africa. For them the closer one gets in mind and taste to the western man, the better one is for all concerned. Even till today the colour line for many of the elite, favours light skins and there is often an unspoken preference for lighter skins amongst Africans. Your know as well as I do how much skin bleaching especially in the face still goes on amongst Africans, particularly our womanhood. This is largely a reflection of the fact that in correspondence with the legacy of the colonial heritage, many Africans see the white man's colour in superior terms. The darker you are, as the underlying assumption runs, the closer you are to primitivism. Many would deny this, but our social practice in Africa speaks more loudly than empty denials. There are others who consider such matters virtually too touchy and raw to be broached in discussion, and who regard the airing of such views as being in bad taste. But I am convinced that unless and until such time that we are willing and able to confront and discuss such matters openly and freely, our chances of gaining self-respect, self-assertiveness, and the ability to integrate our history and culture relevantly into our present concerns would be elusive. It needs to be said that, an awakened Africa cannot be built on a bankrupt culture, we need to clean up the mess of the present, rehabilitate our culture as part of the national democratic transformational process, in which post-colonial Africa is immersed.

In essence there is light at the end of the tunnel for during the last two decades many of us have gone through the traumatic experience of moving from the transient euphoria of the early independence years to the disillusionment of the seventies and eighties. Today it has become increasingly clear that our generation in Africa could serve as a theoretical and practical bridge between the beginnings of the collapse of neo-colonialism and the emergence of novel structures and institutions, for the struggle for the completion of the process of the African national and democratic transformation, emancipation, and total independence.

The national democratic movement must unite a broad front of ideas and activity, it must hold together all the social groups opposed to imperialism. For, it needs to be remembered that the fundamental contradiction of our times, is the contradiction against imperialism, internal contradictions are in the main of lesser significance, except when they are distorted and blown out of proportion, by big power influences. Internal contradictions should not be over-presented. We should therefore be careful in rhetoric and practice, not to alienate social groups and elements, which in the process of advancing the national and democratic process have for a considerable historical distance, a progressive and constructive role to play. We must carry on with such social forces, for as long as they have a useful purpose to serve, and not alienate them with language or activity which strikes terror and fear in them, and which on our side would appear quixotic, fanatical or ultra-leftist and divorced from the concrete realities of contemporary social life.

I would now like to say something regarding my thinking on the national and agrarian questions. The agrarian question is the bedrock of the African revolution. We must not oppose those capitalist forms which may be in support of the nascent or rudimentary national accumulative social element in their competition against international interests. Rather we should encourage and carry them along in as far as their activities are in opposition to the dominance and autonomous operations of international finance. Where international interests expand the growth of local productive forces, this should also be encouraged for as long as we dictate the terms.

We need to develop accumulative economic structures premised on African cultural institutions which adapt the principle of the joint-stock company to suit our historical and cultural usages on an inter-African level, both in the public and private spheres of economic life. The capitalist system both in Africa and the wider world has still life ahead, and I consider it in this day and age, "the socialism of fools" to think that socialism on a world scale is round the corner, or can be voluntaristically selected or rejected, in much the same way that we go to a shop to buy goods. Capitalism was born at a given point in history, as a result of specific historical conditions and class formations, and like everything that is born in history will die a historical death when it is done. That death, much as we will welcome it, when it arrives, is not in immediate view, and therefore we must use the existing system to develop further the productive forces in Africa. I am analytically convinced that socialism will historically supersede capitalism, but that period is not immediately round the corner.

Because of the partition of Africa a century ago, African nationalities were chopped up in bits and pieces, which bear no semblance to the reality of ethnological differentiation of the continent. Borders were drawn up which cut through both agro-ecological zones and nationalities. The result is that throughout the colonial period to the present, the processes of capitalist penetration into pre-capitalist social formations straddle borders in as far as the social classes engendered by these processes are concerned. For example, in the Ivory Coast/Ghana border areas one would find that the same or similar social classes have been formed in the process of cash crop production and the penetration of a cash nexus. The ethnicities involved are the same or ethno-historically proximate. What this implies is that it is easier and historically more relevant to advance or project similar agrarian programmes for democratic reform across borders than within the same country, as we move from one agro-ecological zone, one socio-cultural group, one set of production relations, to the next. Such agrarian reforms would in programming and action dovetail more structurally into the socio-cultural features of the people across borders. Thus in the sphere of ideas, such cross-border programmes would unite peasants around similar agrarian programmes in cultural features and attributes which they share in common. It would reinforce my earlier arguments regarding the need to standardize other cultural attributes principally languages.

I know simple minds are apt to interpret this argument as some sort of latter day version of apartheid. This is certainly not what I am saying. I am not suggesting that agrarian programmes at the material base, and socio-cultural intercourse at the ideological level should create hermetically sealed enclaves, based on ethnicity and inequality. What I am saying is that we should proceed along lines which build on the historical, socio-economic and cultural conditions of the African masses, while keeping open all avenues for interrelations between the various nationalities, on the basis of democracy in an economic, social, and cultural sense. Once we understand that this is to be achieved under the umbrella of wider African unity and not separateness of any kind, the gist of the argument becomes clearer, I hope. We would need to create institutions which cut across our borders as they currently stand. Institutions which unite our people across borders. Needless to say our indigenous languages in standardized forms would be crucial for the ideological success of this approach. This approach would ensure that our nationalities are rehabilitated in a form which subsumes existing state borders and, if this is placed within the wider matrix of the Pan-Africanist framework, then the sort of ethnic divisions, and chauvinist inspired ethnic conflict (tribalism) would be obliterated, or reduced to oblivion.

In effect, I am saying that, Pan-Africanism is the answer against tribalism. Furthermore, Pan-Africanism, in order to be put on a firm rational footing would need to tackle directly the national and agrarian questions. When the Pan-Africanists demand land in South Africa, they are demanding, what was taken from them, in many instances, only 75 years ago. Contemporary realities demand a subtle and pragmatic approach which does not damage the economy, but the principle cannot be denied.

Because African states cannot deal with the heritage of African culture and history, they regard with suspicion bordering on paranoia, any expression of cultural identity, especially since they realise too well that, nationalities in Africa straddle borders in almost all instances right across the continent. Instead of recognising the historical and cultural characteristics of our people and giving them a democratic socio-structural form which could serve to unite our people across borders, in order to protect their interests and the interests of their masters, they clobber any expression of African socio-cultural forms, as backward, primitive and tribalistic. Once we understand that standardized African language groups would not be pitted against each other, but rather brought together under a wider umbrella of African unity and Pan-Africanism, the fear of this should be removed.

This fear is currently still present and not removed on account of the fact that African ruling groups pay only lip-service to the idea of unity. The ruling groups do not really want unity, they accept the results of the partition of Africa and are desperate in their efforts to make the European-bestowed identities of the present stick. They fail to see that Africans, in their culture and history have existed from time immemorial. We are not creations of the westerner. We existed long before the westerner arrived in Africa, and will exist long after they have as overlords left Africa to its own destiny.

I am happy to say that in a way, our generation has "discovered" Africa. Thirty to forty years ago, you could easily count the numbers of West Africans in East or Southern Africa or vice versa. Today we are interacting and mingling in an unprecedented fashion, in ways which are acceptable and other ways which are despicable. But, that is the nature of dialectics. It is all part of the historical process. In any case we have started to find each other, not only in mind, but also very physically. The ferment is on.

Migration and social interaction has slowly started dissolving excessively localist perspectives on life, by the masses. Localist and regionalist notions are still very prevalent and unfortunately for most of the time this is hardly understood as a positive, possible, democratic socio-psychological sentiment, with possibilities for economic institutions which could assist the process of the development of the productive forces in Africa across borders. We must exploit our common cultural heritage, large language areas, which as I have earlier said need to be standardized, with of course the structural tolerance for dialectal and phonological diversity. That way we would open the channels for the masses to understand science and technology in their own historico-culturally natural idioms. We would have created from that point on, a situation in which a decade later we could have science and technology firmly implanted at the village level. This is certainly something we cannot do with English, French or Portuguese.

My experience in Africa, having lived and worked in nine countries has revealed to me, what I describe as the phenomenon of the "foreign native". He or she is one of the most miserable humans you can think of. I need to let you know that the term "foreign native" is not original to me. I am borrowing it, tongue in cheek, from the language of the Apartheid administrators, who used it to describe any African from north of the Limpopo river working in South Africa, as migrant labour. I use it rather humouristically to laugh at myself and Africans like myself, living and working outside the neocolonial states of their birth. Local natives appear to feel some sort of competitive antagonism towards the "foreign native" breed. In any working situation for the "foreign native" it is wiser to curb ambition, shun seniority or the limelight. This is in itself understandable. It is however the difference in reaction to other foreigners which makes it a particularly interesting phenomenon. The worst victims are Africans from states adjacent or most proximate. Generally the further your origins as an African, the more welcome you are. Africans are fundamentally very welcoming and responsive to other Africans from distant African countries. What is particularly sad is the fact that we welcome, bow and scrape to nationals from all other continents, but reserve our worst reception to are own brothers and sisters, especially the most immediate. It is actually a syndrome and result of oppression. Centuries of oppression has cultivated in the African, self-hatred. The African today, if I may generalize, despises him or herself, admires the European, and anything lighter than him or herself.

The African continent today is inhabited principally by two large nations; the African and the Arab. Among those groups are to be found many different nationalities and sub-nationalities. As I have earlier said, there are also other nationalities of non-African origins, who now belong to Africa, in an existential sense. African society and culture have on the whole been greatly enriched by the cultures which these groups represent. For as long as equal cultural and political rights are accorded all, free of discrimination on the basis of colour or creed, and furthermore, that there are no institutions barring the free flow of people and ideas across nationality and ethnic lines, with the freedom to join others and to preserve what one wishes to preserve, nothing reactionary can emerge in the face of the deepening emancipatory and democratic process. I think however that, the problem as we move to the close of the twentieth century would be the issue of the Afro-Arab borderlands. This matter would need to be resolved with again an eye on collective and democratic decision-making, ultimately supporting democratic processes for Arab unity but opposing expansionism, while championing African unity and rejecting national chauvinism. The day the border between Africa and the Arab world is drawn to the satisfaction of the masses on both sides of the border based on democratic principles, that day our vision of African unity would have arrived virtually at our doorstep.

Regarding the 7th Pan-African Congress and generally what is to be done, I would like to note that we should avoid excessive formalism in our organisational tactics. We should in as far as it is possible, allow practice to advice our organizational structures. Let us operate within the mass movement, guiding it from within. Concretely, the 7th Pan-African Congress should:

a)   Define who an African is.

b)   Scientifically summarize the experience of the past.

c)   Formulate and adopt a programme of action for the future.

d)   Agree on a democratic basis for the calling of Congresses. In other words, provide the institution with a democratic base.

e)   Put in place institutional and organizational structures for the achievement of our objectives based on clear democratic principles.

f)   Address the problem of the Afro-Arab borderlands.

g)   Define our position on the national rights of the diaspora.

There are those who would point to, either for or against, my usage of marxian analytical notions, however unorthodox. I regard that approach to the analysis of social and historical processes as methodologically unrivalled even in this day and age, when so many are afraid to say so, or have abandoned previously held positions. I have never in spite of my usage of this approach been a faithful regurgitator of Novosti Press or Pravda; or regarded the views of Marx in all respects with Biblical finality. The Soviet Empire has never impressed me, and about a quarter of a century ago, I resigned my position as Secretary-General of GHANASO (Ghana National Students Organization) on account of their gross manipulation of the Ghanaian youth movement, which some of my colleagues were prepared to accept. I share Richard Wright's sentiments made known some 40 years ago in this respect, although, I do not agree with his wider and other views associated with him, in many respects;

> ...my utilization of Marxist instrumentalities of thought does not necessarily commit me to programmes or policies popularly associated with Marxist philosophy. The measures which I recommend at the end of this book do not derive from any programmatic theories of any political party. They are derived from my concern about human freedom, from what I know of the world, from what I saw and felt in Africa... (9).

The intellectual influences that have formed me are more than one, and more than I dare list here. I enjoy and relish many things from other non-African cultures, including art, music and literature.

To close, I have this to say for myself. I am African first and all other identities second. It is a position which has taken me some time to reach but for which I am today in my mind a much happier and stronger person. Being Ghanaian is for me secondary to being an African. The latter subsumes the former. I am confident in my mind that the cause of African unity will triumph in the end. It is not going to be easy or a bed or roses but as is often said, "there is no easy walk to freedom". Because the struggle for African emancipation, freedom and unity is tied to the democratic struggle of humankind I am sure there is victory for us. We must support democratic processes wherever they may be. This can only support our own freedom and unity.

Notes

1. C. L. Sulzberger. *The Last of the Giants*. London. 1972. pp.302-303.

2. S.R.B. Attoh Ahuma. *The Gold Coast Nation and National Consciousness*. Liverpool. 1911.

3. "The Notion of Cultural Blockage and Some Issues of Science and Technology, Concerning the African Peasantry". In, *K.K.Prah (ed). Culture, Gender, Science and Technology in Africa*. Windhoek. 1991.

4. Kobina Sekyi. "The Future of Subject Peoples". In, *The Africa Times and Orient Review. October-December 1917*. Quoted here from *J. Ayo Langley. Ideologies of Liberation in Black Africa*. London. 1979. p 250.

5. Mary Kingsley's view was quoted by Kuye, as it is presented in Edward Blyden's African Life and Customs. John Williamson Kuye. "The Right of People to Self-Determination. With Special Reference to British West Africa". In, *The Gambia Outlook and Senegambia Reporter. Nos.7 and 21. November 1936*. Quoted here from *J. Ayo Langley*, Ibid. p.216.

6. J. E. Casely Hayford. *Ethiopia Unbound*. 1908. Quoted here from J. Ayo Langley. Ibid. p 204. Ayo Langley (Ibid. p 14) has rightly drawn attention to the need to avoid "facile political analogies" between Japan and Africa. This cannot be disputed especially since he mentions the fact that; "there would have been no objection if the analogies were supported by historical; or statistical data". The point must however not be overstated. Japan remains one shining example of a non-western country which has made a tremendous success of the use of its indigenous culture as a base for incomparable societal advancement. All of this is largely a post-Meiji phenomenon. The key lesson of the Japanese case is that technological advancement must be premised on an indigenous cultural base. This is a point which was well understood by the Sarbahs, Casely Hayford and other African nationalists in the late 19th and early 20th century. See my; Colonized Attitudes in the Gold Coast Before the Russo-Japanese War. In, K.K.Prah. *Essays on African Society and History*. Ghana Universities Press. Accra. 1975.

7. George Padmore. *Pan-Africanism or Communism?* London. 1955. p. 118.

8. W.E.B. Du Bois. *The Pan African Movement*. Quoted here from, *E. Kedourie (ed). Nationalism in Asia and Africa*. London. 1971. pp.372-373.

9. Richard Wright. *Black Power*. London. 1954. p.3.

The Diaspora as Host

Cape Town
27.1.94.

Dear Friend,

We are trying to organise the 8th Pan-African Congress (PAC) or something to that effect, not necessarily with that series in the name. I don't know whether you heard about the 7th Pan-African Congress, which was held in Kampala in April 1994, or if you heard about it, what the whole thing came across to you as being about. It turned out to be a huge jamboree of "Pan-African church men and women" coming to a shrine to swear allegiance to a faith they vaguely and unfortunately for too many in a millenarian fashion adhere to, without care for what they socially and substantially uphold. There were some very "spiritually" ecstatic moments, but unfortunately these emotional lifts were not underscored in any historical sense by intellectual ballast. We had a great deal of "fine speeches", name-dropping and stage management. There was an inability to advance the course of the emancipation of people of African descent in any sensible or theoretically enlightening way. This was largely because from a very early and preparatory stage, the whole project, or if you like jamboree, and its object, was highjacked by elements and minds which were more concerned with the dramatics of seeing the "7th Pan-African Congress" than people who were anxious to midwife a qualitative development in the intellectual underpinnings of the struggle for the emancipation of people of African descent. I hope the next chapter of this process delivers more gold. We cannot go back to that sort of "nigger heaven" and political posturing.

The idea which some of us are pushing is that the next instalment of the development of ideas for African emancipation should be hosted by the diaspora, in the United States of America. The advantages could be enormous. Needless to say there are also possible pitfalls.

Firstly, the sort of interference and moral high-grounding which

African state authorities, would assume in theory and practice would be avoided. A meeting like I am suggesting cannot take place anywhere in Africa, without the local authorities attempting to hijack or bend it to suit their own narrow intentions. The United States authorities may be interested in knowing what we have to say and what we are doing, but they can never deny its democratic intent and content. For this reason, I suspect (rather vaguely and maybe naively) that, it would be allowed, without them interfering, or wanting to interfere too closely. We have nothing to hide about our struggle for emancipation. If they have any sense, they would welcome this as part of the broad progress of homo sapiens. America is in the leadership of today's world and must accept the responsibilities thereof. They may be unhappy with a process beyond their control, but then the conceptualization of the historical destiny of human freedom and democracy is not anybody or state's monopoly.

Anyway, let me go back to more pressing issues. Secondly, the convention of such a meeting in North America will expose the lie of the argument that the premise of the definition of African people is based on what I call "continentalism" or colour. Why do I say this? All African people are identifiable, directly or indirectly, to the present continent of Africa. Most African people are obviously black both on the continent and in the diaspora, but not all African people are black. Not all Black people are African. There are Blacks who are Jews and others who are Arabs. Chinese are not Arabs, nor are Europeans, Indians. When we say African people, to my simple mind, we are referring to those whose historical and/or cultural origins are African, from the African continent, and whose sense of identity as understood and recognized by themselves is rooted in Africa. Thus the diaspora is African whilst the Arab peoples on the north of the continent are not.

There are people whose origins are rooted in Africa, who till today, do not accept their primary identification with Africa and who prefer other historical characterisations, although they are citizens of African countries. They may in due course come to see themselves as part of us. They are, and should always be, treated in citizenship rights as African citizens, but should not be forced or imposed upon to identify themselves as historically or culturally African. They have and must always have the right to identify themselves as they wish. I am not in favour of forcibly bestowing African identity on people who do not see themselves fundamentally as Africans, and maybe rightfully so. By the same token, I think it is inappropriate to regard Native Australians and Western Samoans and Papua New Guineans or Dravidian Indians as Africans simply because they are black.

Our arguments have always been free of the sort of anti-human assumptions which derive the definition of peoples primarily on the basis of colour. Ironically, being black is only a bonus we have. In the absence of points of solidarity based on religious commonality, geographical unity in a total sense and linguistic homogeneity, colour becomes for us for obvious reasons of the high and distinctive visibility it provides, an extra and fortunate point of reference. In this sense, as I have elsewhere said, we are extraordinarily lucky for our colour. It is a reason for which we have incredibly suffered. But, we have also remarkably survived our suffering, and our existential triumph inspite of our suffering remains today for the witness of humankind a source of great inspiration.

I like to remind people of the fact that following the Vietnamese nationalist, Ho Chi Minh's visit to West Africa, the second decade of this now-dying century, he made the remark that "it is a well known fact that the African people are the most oppressed of humankind". We still live with this reality, whether on the Continent or in our diaspora. My hope is that our next PAC, the 8th or whatever we call it (an All-African Peoples Congress), will come to terms with the notion of a unified nationhood. Who are we? My argument has always been that "if everybody is an African, then nobody is an African", and how crucial is our freedom, in a wide sense, for the development of human civilisation? If we are as a nation "the wretched of the earth" then logically the movement for our freedom is a crucial and vital ingredient for human freedom as a universal, historically incremental project.

Arab slavery still continues on the African continent. Furthermore, throughout the Afro-Arab borderlands the Arabisation process of Africans is being pursued in some instances as a matter of state

65

policy. You know, or will recall the case of the Sudan, or Mauritania for that matter. I should maybe, for example, draw your attention to some of the painful details which so many people in discussions regard as taboo. People are inclined to tip-toe around the issue and hope that by avoiding it, it somehow disappears or ceases to exist. It is considered to be an issue to be avoided in polite conversation and in public meetings, anybody raising this issue is regarded with distaste. I am disgusted by the hypocrisy of this attitude, which refuses to confront the realities of African slavery by Arabs in the contemporary world, in the Afro-Arab borderlands.

In 1987, Ushari Ahmed Mahmud and Suleyman Ali Baldo in a paper entitled *Human Rights Abuses in the Sudan (1987)* revealed that;

> In May-June 1987 we were investigating the Diein massacre. While interviewing the survivors, they told us about the existence of slavery in the area and we decided to investigate that, too. Thus far we have received information and strong evidence that slavery, in its classical and known sense, has re-emerged in the Sudan.... In the following section, we present extracts from recorded interviews with Dinka men, women, and a child. These persons had been affected by slavery in different ways: one woman had seen children and women enslaved in Diein, and her own infant was kidnapped during the massacre. A policeman reports of a Dinka woman who came to the police station in Diein complaining that her son had been enslaved by a particular person. A Dinka man has made it his duty to free Dinkas from slavery. Another man tells of the sale of his brother. An old woman tells how the Rizeigat and another tribe attacked her village and kidnapped 11 of her relatives.

Rakyia Omar, the Somali jurist and human rights activist, former director of *Africa Watch*, a couple of years ago sent me some damning material of a similar kind on Mauritania. I seriously regard it as an insult against my intelligence to be searching for modes of unity with people who from time immemorial, to the present day, continue to hold us in slavery. I am, of course not, in any way disregarding or under-playing the expressed wish of articulate and democratic minds in the Arab world for Arab unity. But, this, obviously, to such minds is more fundamental and primary than African unity. Their aspiration is toward Arab unity. The latter is a democratic principle which all freedom-loving people in the world should support in much the same way as we must support the democratic process of European unity, but uncompromisingly, we have the same right. I cannot see how one could subsume the intentions and aspirations of African unity to the objectives of the Arab League. What I mean is that one is either struggling for African unity in Africa, or Arab unity.

We need a serious meeting to deal with these and other related issues. I hope that you can assist with identifying about 8 academicians and others in the U.S. who are proven Pan-Africanists (not just informed academics or students of Pan-Africanism) to serve as a Planning Committee that will assist with organising an international Congress of Pan-Africanists in the U.S. This Congress should take place in 1997, giving us about two years to organise. The Planning Committee will become part of a larger, more representative (geographically and ideologically) Steering Committee that will draft the Call and other supportive working document(s). I am prepared to draft a working paper, which I will send to Steering Committee members for their comments, additions and subtractions. The final product can serve as the basis for developing the Programme for the Congress. I trust that you will reply as soon as your schedule permits.

Beyond the Colour Line, The Language of Pan-Africanism and the Pan-Africanism of Language

Presented to the Conference on; Africa and the World (Dept. of History, University of Manchester); Fiftieth Anniversary of the 1945 Manchester Pan-African Congress. 13th to 15th October 1995.

Introduction:

As we race towards the close of this century and indeed the millennium, humanity is challenged amongst other things, by the relative backwardness of Africa and its peoples. In politics as well as culture, Asian peoples in especially the Far East and South East Asia have emerged out of colonial tutelage to become dragons in the global economy. In places like Indonesia, Malaysia, Singapore, over the past decade and a half, economic and social development has been phenomenal. Korea, Taiwan/China and Mainland China are entering the next century with an economic big-bang. In the next decade we shall see in all probability a challenge to Western economic hegemony. In much of Asia, Asian capitalism has long replaced Western dominance. Asian capital has in turn partly moved west. Asia has been westernized, but on its own terms. Asia has by and large found the route to a selective adoption of western ideas without subverting the core of its cultural base.

There are important differences between the East which met the West, and the Africa which encountered Europe. Asia confronted colonialism with in many parts literate cultures with religious systems of routinized priesthood. Especially south of the north, African religious systems, shamanistic and illiterate as they were, shared a degree of similarity across the continent which is incomparable to any other similar geographical spread in the world. African religious practices became heathen first after the Arab conquest of North Africa. A thousand odd years later, European Christian colonial interests introduced their own heathenizing ideology in the quest to control Africans. Except amongst the preliterate cultures of Asia

68

western colonialism ran into a wall protecting the cultural world of the Asiatic as a Muslim, Hindoo, Buddhist, Confucian, or Shintoist. The preliterate cultures of Africa were more vulnerable. But what we can say at the end of the 20th century is that, whereas much of the African cultural integument has been eroded, a degree of resilience girded by languages as living forms have maintained a recognizable cultural grid which continues to root the African into history and cultural identity.

Asia's economic miracle is premised on a recognition and use of indigenous languages as a basis of social and economic development. This paper argues that if Africa is to join the march to economic prosperity and the social and economic empowerment of its humanity, it must establish its efforts on its own cultural usages, away from the smothering and suffocating embrace of western economic hegemony and cultural effacement. The cultivation and development of African languages are crucial to this.

The Backdrop

Some years ago during the decade of African independence (1960s), Kohn and Sokolsky remarked that "many observers treat Pan-Africanism as a fanciful phenomenon with little likelihood of attainment, charging it with little more than resolution-passing and flamboyant rhetoric". This view has since then grown among many more, as the euphoria of the period evaporated in the face of entrenched political inertia of the ruling groups unwilling to abandon the material gains of the class ascendancy that the petty bourgeoisie which had led the independence process had gained in the dispensation of the post-colonial state.

The other important contributory factor for this inertia has been the socio-structural constraints imposed by the retreating colonial powers which ensured the maintenance of a neo-colonial political economy and a denationalized hegemonic culture of the elite. An increasingly popular view is also that, even if the inheritance of the colonial order has been neo-colonial as many thoughtful Africans have in recent decades suggested, what are Africans doing about this condition? How are they working to reverse or remove the political and economic legacy of colonialism? Africans cannot, it is pointed out, continue *ad infinitum* to blame others for their own inadequacies, for their own lack of will to address their perceived needs. This societal paralysis, the aura of hopelessness and helplessness deeply invested in African attempts at development betrays an inability for the elite to innovate. It is an elite which is more consummative than innovative, more concessionary than acquisitive. The received colonial culture has remained hegemonic. The African elite is the inheritor of the colonial order but more as a faithful creature than a negation of colonialism. It has sought refuge in national anthems and flags as symbols of sovereignty and pursued the ideals of "nation-building" and the western paradigm of the nation-state on the basis of neocolonial states carved out by the colonial powers some as recently as the 1960s. Fighting over spoils in booty economies, it has raised the status of banana republics to membership of the United Nations.

The beginnings of the demise of the neocolonial African elite is lying before us as we go into the 21st century, the start of a new millennium. In the next two decades, it is likely to go through death throes for which the masses will be responsible, and for which the masses will bear the brunt of a struggle for their social and economic upliftment. The instruments of state power are likely to be challenged in one country after the other as these states fail to deliver the benefits of the economic and social inventions of our times. The tragedies of Rwanda, Burundi, Somalia, Sierra Leone and Liberia, herald the difficult and painful times ahead of us. Negating neocolonialism will involve the cultivation of new democratic structures which relate to the cultures and histories of Africans and which do not treat Africans as mere products of western colonialism.

The argument here is that, the most potent idea for African emancipation is the Pan-Africanist position. It has limitedly already produced significant results in the march forward of what the Dutch sociologist Willem Wertheim once described in his *Evolution and Revolution* as the human "waves of emancipation". It has had also serious theoretical and practical setbacks. If Pan-Africanism is to meet the evolving challenges of our times, it needs to go beyond crass reproduction of former views, some of which are today contextually and sociologically irrelevant. *The view here is that the missing link in the quest for African emancipation, development, democracy and unity, lies with the recentering of African languages at the heart of African endeavours at social transformation.* African progress must be culturally constructed on the basis of the indigenous heritage. African languages are the core of African culture, and culture is the source and essence of identity, not colour. No society in modern times has techno-culturally advanced on the basis of the rejection of its cultural roots, or the indiscriminate borrowing of extraneous institutions. Mass culture in Africa is without doubt constructed in African languages, not the languages of colonial rule. Discussing the European experience, Barbara Ward, in her Plaunt Lectures delivered at Carleton University in 1966 rightly observed:

> What was unique in Western Europe was the thrusting up of new groups and classes to demand effective participation in the political life of the community. If they were to participate, they would have literally "to speak the same language". Literacy, education in greater depth, and the vernacular tongue ended the old split between ruling groups, often speaking an alien language, and the indifferent masses leaving politics to their betters. A community in depth began to form, conscious above all of its language as a bond of unity (2).

Ward was making her point in conjunction with an explanation of the emergence of the European nation-state. The social class implications of the point however remain relevant to contemporary Africa. The use of colonial languages to which present ruling groups in Africa are in practice unflinchingly committed underscores their appendaged and dependent relationship to the old imperial powers and the neocolonial system left in place at the onset of the independence era. It is a relationship which condemns Africans, their culture and history, to an inferior connection in the global scheme of things. If we want to be regarded as equal, and so treated by the rest of humanity, we would need to treat our own as equal in the first instance. Treating our own as equal in this respect is not for sentimental reasons, but rather for the fact that, African social and economic advancement is realizable only if the effort is erected on the basis of African languages and culture.

71

At Home and Abroad

In order to appreciate the grounding of the Pan-Africanist project, it is useful as a point of departure to recall the fact that the idea was born in the African diaspora. The applicability of the term diaspora in this context has been a contested issue. At the heart of the debate is the dispute about the appropriateness or suitability of the concept for the description of Africans taken as slaves across the Atlantic. The term generally excludes those Africans taken into bondage by Arabs and who have generally melted into Middle Eastern Arab society through assimilation. Diaspora, (*Galut*, or *Golah*) as Skinner indicates is generically derived from the Jewish experience. He finds that, "the plight of the people of African descent especially those in the New World is similar to that of the Jews" (3). In Shepperson's estimation, the idea of the "African Abroad", "The African Diaspora" are both factually and as historical commentary related to strands of Judaeo-Christian history. While the term diaspora applied to Africans has vague roots in pre-20th century writing, it gained currency between the mid-50s and mid-60s when the political decolonization of Africa was in full swing (4). Orunu Lara's view is that, "the application of the concept of diaspora as a functional unit... to Africa is only explainable through a linkage with the Greco-Jewish tradition" (5). Harris has pointed out that at the First African Diaspora Studies Institute which gathered at Howard University in 1979, a vocal minority of voices "cautioned against overemphasizing the Jewish relationship" (6). Convergencies and divergencies with the case of the "overseas Chinese" can be argued, and various categories of diasporal Africans are described or describe themselves as Afro-Caribbean, African-American, Afro-Brazilian and Euro-African. In iconoclastic tenor, Tony Martin has suggested that;

> I would like to make a simple, straight-forward suggestion that the term *diaspora* be deleted from our vocabulary, because the term *African diaspora* reinforces a tendency among those writing our history to see the history of African people always in terms of parallels in white history. On this model of thinking Garvey is called a "black Zionist"; George Padmore, a "black revolutionary"; and Du Bois, a "black titan". There are parallels between black

history and white history, of course, but it is unfortunate that blacks do not see our history primarily in its own right. We always seem to be looking for parallels in the experience of other peoples to shape our history. In the old days, other peoples told us we had no history at all; now they acknowledge that we have a history, but only in terms of other peoples' history. So, we should do away with the expression *African diaspora*, because we are not Jews. Let us use some other terminology. Let us speak of the African dispersion, or uprooted Africa as somebody suggested, or scattered Africa (7).

Whichever terminological preferences we may be disposed to, the reality of people of African descent dispersed out of a common historical source, who regard their historical root as a significant reference remains an undeniable truth with which humankind lives. What is important is the service to which such signification is put. If such solidarities are employed in the service of the upliftment of humankind and the broad sweep of human emancipation, its value will prove unquestionable. If however such identities are deployed in the affirmation of narrow, racist, chauvinistic or xenophobic objectives, they will in due course be relegated to the scrapheap of history.

Pan-Africanism has so far proved to be, an indispensable instrument in the struggle for freedom for people of African origins, on both the continent and the diaspora. What were the conditions that prompted its emergence? What historical and sociological peculiarities of the diaspora triggered its birth?

The facts about its history and genesis have been well documented by protagonists like Du Bois, Padmore, Nkrumah, and Ras Makonnen (8). To this list can be added the work of numerous students and scholars of Pan-Africanism like Decraene, Hooker, Geiss, Tevoedjre, Legum and Wallerstein (9).

Both practitioners and students of Pan-Africanism tend to agree that the process of alienation and forced estrangement of Africans from different parts of the continent particularly the west coast, taken as slaves to the western hemisphere, provided the existential crucible for the emergence of the idea. The forcible and violent uprootment and the alienating conditions of new world slavery reinforced the wish to return. The mood of this experience and the longing for a return in mind and spirit, if not in body, has been variously registered in the lyrical inspirations of "the spirituals", by Aime Cesaire in his *Cahier d'un Retour au Pays Natal*, Claude Mckay in his poems, *The Outcast* and *Bondage*, Du Bois in *The Souls of Black Folk,* and more recently the exhortations of Bob Marley the singing voice of Rastafarianism, that, "Africa unite".

The conceptual universe of the Pan-Africanist creed has historically encompassed a range of ideals which have in hierarchy and priority changed with time. These transformations in emphasis have been reflections of the historical and social conditions of the times, and how these impinged upon issues of African freedom. As the Arab proverb goes, "men resemble their times more than they resemble their fathers". The Trinidadian Henry Sylvester Williams, the direct forerunner of Du Bois in the Pan-Africanist movement, and who as General-Secretary had been the key figure behind the first Pan-African Congress in 1900 was in his time concerned with obtaining "true British Status" for all black people in the British Empire. According to Hooker, his belief was that, "a reasoned black petition would elicit satisfactory white response". Hooker adds that, in Bishop Alexander Walters' report of the conference he wrote that, the Conference was designed:

> First, to bring into closer touch with each other the peoples of African descent throughout the world; second, to inaugurate plans to bring about a more friendly relation between the Caucasian and African races; third, to start a movement looking forward to the securing to all African races living in civilized countries their full rights and to promote their business interests. None of this was objectionable, but it had little to do with the anti-imperialist cause, and sounded remarkably assimilationist. Moreover, Africa did not appear to concern them directly (10).

Biology and Culture

In his, *In My Father's House*, Appiah in superb style, presses his exceptional ingenuity and enormous verbal facility to exaggerated and contextually vacuous conclusions. Appiah suggests that both Alexander

Crummell and Du Bois fall prey to racist conceptualization. Crummell is in this respect "inchoate", Du Bois it is contended develops this to an "intrinsically racist" position (11). In my estimation the two are if anything, uncomfortable bedfellows. If Crummell is describably emotive, Du Bois is equally cold and cerebral. Much of the evidence for Appiah's conclusions is drawn in the case of Du Bois from the period spanning, *Conservation of Races* (1897) to *Dusk of Dawn* (1940). Crummell's views date to the 1860s. Crummell regarded "the new world negro" as a returnee, armed with the culture of the west as an instrument of African upliftment. His cultural capitulationism and unstinted preference for English above indigenous African languages has profiled him as an archetype of the westernized elite created in the image of the west, and which is estranged from the culture of mass society. In his, *English Language in Liberia*, which appeared in 1861, Crummell expressed the opinion at length that;

> ....let us speak of the African dialects....there are....definite marks of inferiority connected with them all, which place them at the distance from civilised languages...(a) "They are (Quoting Leighton Wilson) harsh abrupt, energetic, indistinct in enunciation, meagre in point of words...inarticulate nasal and guttural sounds,...few inflections and grammatical forms...". This is his description of Grebo, but it may be taken, I think, as on the whole, correct description of the whole class of dialects...(b).These languages...are characterised by lowness of ideas...the speech of rude barbarians...by brutal and vindictive sentiments...a predominance of animal propensities. (c)...they lack those ideas of virtue, of moral truth, and those distinctions of right and wrong with which we, all our life long, have been familiar. (d)....the absence of clear ideas of Justice, Law, Human Rights and Governmental Order...(e)...These supernal truths...which regulate the lives of Christians, are either entirely absent, or else exist,...in an obscure and distorted manner.

Appiah draws attention to the fact that much of Du Bois's views in the late 19th century did not differ substantially from the prevalent ideas of the period, but does not follow the logic of that fact to its ultimate destination. This being that, Du Bois carried rather heavily and faithfully, the scholastic baggage of his contemporaries especially the deadweight of German Romanticism. Broderick has brought this point out to good effect (12).

Du Bois's ideas on "race" during the 19th century *examined with the hindsight of the 20th century* bore the gross weaknesses of scientific thinking on the issue, characteristic of most thinkers of the time. To assail and flail his understanding of the issue without a balanced social, historical and political contextualization of the argument, is possibly to lapse into a type of ahistoricism not uncommon with technicist linguistic philosophical analyses, which discuss philosophical issues as if they exist in a socio-historical vacuum. It is this socio-historical disembodiment of Du Bois's views which lies at the root of Appiah's analysis of Du Bois, and which disables the potency of his discourse. In, the *Conservation of Races*, basing his views on contemporary authorities, Du Bois writes:

> The final word of science, so far, is that we have at least two, perhaps three, great families of human beings - the whites and Negroes, possibly the yellow race. That other races have risen from the intermingling of the blood of these two. This broad division of the world's races which men like Huxley and Raetzel have introduced as more nearly true than the old five-race scheme of Blumenbach, is nothing more than an acknowledgement that, so far as purely physical characteristics are concerned, the differences between men do not explain all the differences of their history. It declares, as Darwin himself said, that great as is the physical unlikeness of the various races of men, their likenesses are greater, and upon this rests the whole scientific doctrine of human brotherhood (13)

Geographical and biological interpretations of society and behaviour have of course been with us for a long time. Theories of this kind have been handed down from Hippocrates, Vegetius, Aquinas and Bodin with regards to the influence of physical factors, particularly climate on humankind and society. The popularity of such notions was strengthened in the 18th century largely as a result of the work of Montesquieu whose anthropogeographical conclusions on the relationship between environment and collective behavioural characteristics enjoyed currency in the academies of the period. Carl Linnaeus who is credited with the first attempts to offer a scientific classification of humans into "racial" sub-divisions focused his attention on assumed behavioural characteristics. The European was described as "light, lively and inventive" while Africans were considered to be "cunning, slow, and negligent".

The direct antecedents of the German tradition which affected Du Bois's formation can be traced to Herder. In his remarkable text *Ideas for the Philosophy of the History of Humanity*, he blended Rousseau's emphasis on the state of nature and primordial freedom, Voltaire's views on national character, and Montesquieu's dialectic of environment and collective behaviour and character. Fichte was even more representative of German idealism. In his *Addresses to the German Nation* (1807), he argued that it was with the German people, that the hope of the future lay. They were for Fichte, an *Urfolk*, a pure or classical "race", an unmixed race, endowed with, "hidden and inexhaustible springs of spiritual life and power". For Fichte, the Romance people were a *Mischfolk*, a mixed or "impure race" (14). Du Bois recounts a stunning experience as a student in Berlin:

> I can never forget that morning in the class of the great Heinrich Von Treitschke in Berlin … his words rushed out in a flood: "Mulattoes", he thundered, "are inferior". I almost felt his eyes boring into me, although probably he had not noticed me. "Sie fuhlen sich niedriger!". "Their actions show it", he asserted. What contradiction could there be to that authoritative dictum? (15).

Du Bois was abreast with the current theories of the late 19th century. His references to "impulses and stirrings" which by implication biologise culture and in effect contradict the culture concept were not far removed from the notions of *volksgeist* common then in the discourses of contemporary western anthropological psychology. To argue on the basis of these postulations that Du Bois was basically racist in the sense that the term is understood in the 20th century constitutes intellectual "presentism" of a misleading kind. The fascistic, Hitlerian and Verwoerdian philosophical position of the 20th century has been a manifestly pernicious anti-human argument.

There are undoubtedly inconsistencies in Du Bois's position, especially the inability during his early period to draw a sharp line between biology and culture. But this was true for most 19th century thinkers. He was an authentic creature of his times and his mentors including Crummell. The fact that his ideas bore so closely the imprint of his period is hardly surprising. It would have been extremely phenomenal if he would at that time stood far ahead of contemporary science and knowledge. His superb biographer David Levering Lewis (1993) in the best biography of Du Bois which has so far appeared (*W.E.B. Du Bois: Biography of a Race 1868-1919*) writes that,

> Great confusion set in at this point, as the young professor wove back and forth between the subjects of English parliamentarianism and free trade, German excellence in science and philosophy, French and Italian fecundity in music, art, and literature, and the contributions of the "other race groups", hopelessly entangling nationality with race and institutions with cultural "traits". Just exactly what race was Du Bois never did manage to say clearly, although he invoked the authorities Thomas Huxley and Friedrich Ratzel in support of his conviction that there were three primordial examples - white, Negro, and yellow, and eight "historic" ones - Teutons, Slavs, English of Great Britain and North America, "Romance nations", Negroes of Africa and America, Semites, Hindus, and Mongolians...... (p. 171)

Seen from the present, with the knowledge and insights that we have today these views appear seriously tainted and enormously flawed. They are opinions which have been rejected by time and intellect and have furthermore been responsible in the twentieth century for much harm in the relations between our human community. Du Bois's inadequacies in this respect are considerable and must rightfully be subjected to criticism.

He can however not be classed as the other side of the coin, in letter or spirit, with sentiments like Bagehot's denigration of "unfit men and beaten races", Lords Cromer and Rosebery's attitudes to "the

Kwak Kwaks and the Kuk Kuks"; Jules Cambon's racist paternalism in Algeria which sought for Muslim Algerians, to "raise their moral and intellectual standards"; or Joseph Gallieni's concept of the *politique des races,* which was enforced in Madagascar (16). Stoecker has drawn attention to the fact that late 19th century Germany was a hotbed of anti-black racism. From the mid-1890s onwards, Social Darwinist assumptions were ascendant. The notion of the; "immutable inferiority of all coloured peoples, particularly Negroes", compared with white men, i.e. Europeans, was virtually unchallenged (17). Most of the ingredients for these views had been concocted throughout the western world. "All that the German bourgeoisie needed to do was to take over the racialist ideas that had been current in Britain (Hamilton Smith, Knox, Hunt), the USA (Morton, Nott, Gliddon) and France (Gobineau) since the 1840s and 1850s and had been used to defend the practice of slavery and colonial subjugation of Africans and people of African descent. These ideas had particular currency in the USA" (18). Ludwig Schemann's work and H.S. Chamberlain's *Die Grundlagen des 19. Jahr-hunderts,* which appeared at the turn of the century were additional contributions to this racist lore. The Social Darwinism of Gumplowicz and Ratzenhofer affirmed this tradition. The confusion of biology with culture in the study of Africans and African society continued into the 20th century. In no lesser a figure as Seligman's work *Races of Africa* which appeared in 1930, he mixes up biological and cultural categories. Boonzaier has rightly suggested that, the real and significant turning point in this racist mystification came in a serious way only in the 1950s under the auspices of UNESCO (19).

The late 19th century was the heyday of western imperialism. The ideas that were rampant in the guise of scientific knowledge served well the emergent colonial enterprise. According to Stoecker, even the German monarch Wilhelm II indulged in rabble-rousing speeches invoking the spectre of "the yellow peril" (20). Needless to say, Du Bois's voice was throughout his life pitched on behalf the downtrodden people of the human race especially those of African descent. He saw his life mission as the task of articulating and organizing activity geared towards their emancipation. In his *Credo,* which Foner points out was originally used in his speeches, but which appeared first in print in 1904, the text opens with the proclamation:

> I believe in God who made of one blood all races that dwell on earth. I believe that all men, black and brown, and white, are brothers, varying, through Time and Opportunity, in form and gift and feature, but differing in no essential particular, and alike in soul and in the possibility of infinite development (21).

Elsewhere Du Bois writes:

> Race would seem to be a dynamic and not a static conception, and the typical races are continually changing and developing, amalgamating and differentiating ... We are studying the history of the darker part of the human family, which is separated from the rest of mankind by no absolute physical line and no definite mental characteristics, but which nevertheless forms, as a mass, a series of social groups more or less distinct in history, appearance and in cultural gifts and accomplishment (22).

August Meier in sympathetic vein, and more consistently sensitive and cautious, than Appiah, to the socio-historical context of late 19th century America writes:

> Like his racist contemporaries, he was certain of the universality of "the race spirit" which he regarded as "the greatest invention for human progress". Each race had a special ideal - the English individualism, the German philosophy and science, and so forth. Therefore, "only Negroes bound and welded together, Negroes inspired by one vast ideal, can work out in its fullness the great message we have for humanity". To those who argued that their only hope lay in amalgamating with the rest of the American population, he admitted that Negroes faced a "puzzling dilemma". Every thoughtful Negro had at some time asked himself whether he was American, or a Negro, or if he could be both; whether by striving as a Negro he was not perpetuating the very gulf that divided the two races, or whether Negroes "have in America a distinct mission as a race". Du Bois's answer was what is now

called cultural pluralism. Negroes were American by birth, in language, in political ideas, and in religion. But any further than this, their Americanism did not go (23).

Notions like the "race spirit" seen as "the greatest invention for human progress" closely echo Hegel. For Hegel, in his *The Philosophy of History*; "the German spirit is the spirit of the new world. Its aim is the realization of absolute Truth as the unlimited self-determination of freedom - that freedom which has its own absolute form itself as its purport". Du Bois was very much a product of his age and was deeply affected by the dominant ideas of his times. What is however remarkable is that his views evolved with time, shedding intellectual garbage and steadily acquiring refinement. In later years his intellectual evolution took him to a polished marxian and internationalist position similar to Paul Robeson's. But even in this respect, there is no evidence to suggest that he was a dogmatist, or a fellow-traveller faithful to the orthodoxy of the Soviet Union, as so many of his contemporaries and near contemporaries became.

The Coordinates of Pan-Africanism
In its most generalized sense, Pan-Africanism is an ideology for the emancipation of African people or people of African descent, on the continent and in the diaspora. It has never been espoused as a credo for the domination or political exclusion of non-African peoples. In this respect, it differs radically from the Herrenvolk ideas of Hitlerian Germany, the Baaskap philosophy of Apartheid, or the sentiments which inform the myth "Britannia Rules the Waves". The fact that most Africans or people of African descent are black does not make the Pan-Africanist argument racist, this is the extended import of Du Bois point that, "the black man is a man who must ride 'Jim Crow' in Georgia" (24). In Africa throughout this century and long before, he or she is the person who took instructions from and served other human beings, who happen to be white. In the language of the Calvinist South African whites, the African as descendant of Ham is the hewer of wood and drawer of water. The African as a social, historical or cultural product, or black person as a crude classification

81

of skin pigmentation invariably overlap. This is not because history and colour are factually interchangeable categories, but because Africans taken into bondage in the new world were black. In the above respects, in the specific social contexts in which these identifications find meaning they are also preeminently a class category. If you organized victims of Jim Crow treatment in Georgia fifty years ago they would all have turned out to be black. But, that would not make that a racist movement. My old friend Sivanandan, in a letter to the *Encounter (July 1968)*, in a style brimming with indignation and strident eloquence wrote;

> ... to the black man his colour is a whole way of life, of non-life. To say that he is colour conscious is to imply that he has been allowed the possibility of another consciousness. In fact, it would be truer to say that his colour is the one thing he does not wish to be conscious of - for it is his mark of oppression. He has tried to escape it as best as he could; aping the white man, playing the white man's game (even when he changed the rules so as to keep on winning), even forcing the white man to concede a victory or two.

In the real world of today and yesterday, in Africa and the western hemisphere, people of African descent have been more the victims of racism than the theoretical and practical champions of racism. Racism is a power relationship; a social and ideological construction which raises superficial biological attributes to objects and markers for social and economic dominance or subordination. Its intellectual baseness, crudity and grossness is such that even simple animals as dogs are free from such fictions of the mind. In Jean-Paul Sartre's persuasive analysis of the psycho-pathology of the Anti-Semite, *Anti-Semite and Jew*, he writes in one of his concluding paragraphs, "I am told a Jewish league against Anti-Semitism has just been reconstituted. I am delighted; that proves that the sense of authenticity is developing among the Jews". His hope however was that other people would join this endeavour, since the triumph of the crusade against anti-Semitism is a triumph of humanity as a whole. Slaves whose terms of enslavement are partly defined on the basis of skin colour by the master cannot be accused of racism against their overlords, if in resistance, such slaves organize themselves as people of colour against slavery. Any discussion of Pan-Africanism which in effect attempts to turn the victims of western racism into protagonists is in this day intellectually ill-conceived and could be construed by some to be mischievous. When Africans and people of African descent attempt to organize or rationalize their resistance to oppression these realities need to be borne in mind. Occasion has elsewhere provided scope for the statement:

> The racial definition of an African is flawed. It is unscientific and hence untenable. No serious mind today would use the race concept in any way except as an instrument for poetic imagery. What I am saying is that no group of people has been "pure" from time immemorial. Notions of purity belong to the language of fascists and the rubbish-bin of science. But before my observations are misunderstood let me take the argument into another direction. Most Africans are black, but not all Africans are black, and not all blacks have African cultural and historical roots. Jews range from blond to black. Another example, Arabs also do (25).

If the problem of the twentieth century has been the problem of the colour line, the 21st century, takes us beyond the colour line into a new world where cultural coexistence and democracy determine how we survive together as humanity in a shrinking global village. The Pan-Africanist position needs to define its grounding in historical and cultural terms which are emancipatory for mass society, and which in object does not contradict or deny the rights of other people. I am arguing that, any definition of the freedom of any people or group, which in theory and practice pans out in the proscription or disavowal of the freedom of other groups is in principle and practice objectionable.

The component of the Pan-Africanist idea which stresses the goal of political unity can be seen as an instrument for the emancipation process. Its emphatic articulation and centrality in the ideological preoccupations of Pan-Africanists is of relatively younger age than the colonization ventures and "back to Africa" movements of the 19th century and the 20th century best exemplified by the Garveyist UNIA

(Universal Negro Improvement Association) undertaking. From the late 18th century through the 19th century, the "back to Africa" and colonization school was the dominant opinion amongst proto-Pan-Africanists. The creation of Liberia, Sierra Leone and the return of Afro-Brazilians who settled in small pockets along the whole of the West Africa coast was a direct result of these ideas. Garvey's movement was the highwater mark of the "back to Africa" and colonization tradition. The most important impact of his movement was that it gave confidence to people who had for too long been made to accept and feel inferior. The effects of his ideas on the African independence movement has tended to be underestimated. From west to south and eastern Africa during the 20s and 30s Garvey's ideas greatly inspired Africans on the continent. In Kwame Nkrumah's autobiography, he writes, "... of all the literature I studied (as a student in the USA during the 1930s) the book that did more than any other to fire my enthusiasm was the *Philosophy and Opinions of Marcus Garvey*". It is also important to note that, Garvey's movement stirred the hearts and minds of the lower classes amongst blacks, in a way that no other movement had hitherto done. In this respect, Garvey galvanized the hoi polloi in a way that Du Bois's contemporary efforts could not achieve.

With regards to the work and ideas of Du Bois, it was only after 1945, when with the entrance of people like Nkrumah and Kenyatta, these ideas became part of the mass movement for independence in Africa that they made a difference in practice. In a related fashion, ideas like "Negritude" and "African Personality" in themselves were meaningless in the lives of the masses. They were in fact populist notions reflective of petty bourgeois positions. They were however significant in as far as they posed a counterpoint to the cultural and psychological effects of colonialism and western racism. This is why Sartre's description of "antiracist racism" makes sense, but only just, because to suggest that Negritude is racism is to attribute to a reaction to racism, racism. Sartre is however perceptive in his dialectic when he suggests in the *Black Orpheus* that this "antiracist racism" will dialectically negate western racism and lead ultimately to the abolition of racial differences. The full meaning of this point appears to be lost on Appiah. In his, *The Third World*, Peter Worsley criticizing Colin Legum makes a point similar to the argument here. He writes;

> *Negritude*, in fact, does not, as Colin Legum suggest, rest, "deep at its quivering, sensitive centre.... on colour consciousness...", rather, colour consciousness is itself an expression of the colonial experience, and to the common fate of the Black man under imperialism.

Worsley is spot on. This is a point which must not be overlooked.

Many of the British colonial forces drawn from the West Indies who fought in the wars of "pacification" at the early stages of the establishment of British colonial rule stayed. Towards the closing stages of the 19th century, largely through the inspiration of the ideas of Edward Blyden and James Africanus Horton, slowly the views of people like Sarbah.Snr, Casely-Hayford, Holy Johnson, Macauley, Sarbah.Jnr, and Attoh-Ahuma came into the picture and placed emphasis on self-rule, cultural assertiveness, and unity if even under colonial tutelage.

During the late 1930s, particularly at the time of the Abyssinian Crisis, the intellectual shift towards colonial freedom seriously emerged. Figures like Kenyatta, Cab Kaye, George Padmore, C.L.R. James and Ras Makonnen became active in the intellectual gestation of this process in the UK (26). It was at this time that, C.L.R. James formed the International Africa Friends of Ethiopia. The significance of the Manchester 1945 Conference, lies in the fact that African independence shifted to the top of the agenda of Pan-Africanists. From Manchester the plans for colonial freedom went out. A mere decade after Manchester, Ghana stood at the door of political independence. The All Africa Peoples Conference of 1958 in Accra set the pace for the work of Lumumba, Banda, Nkomo and others.

The agenda for political unity became both theoretically and practically pregnant after Ghana's independence in 1957. What was to happen after colonial freedom became the question of the time. This was the point in Nkrumah's well-known statement pronounced on the occasion of Ghana's independence that, "the independence of Ghana is meaningless unless it is linked with the total liberation of Africa".

It is noteworthy that, during the late 1950s and early 1960s, Pan-Africanists envisaged the newly independent states to be the building-blocks of a unified Africa. Nkrumah and Cheikh Anta Diop attempted variously to give detail to these ideas. Quaison-Sackey's *Africa Unbound*, which provides a graphic account of the very early attempts at creating unity through the amalgamation of the newly independent countries, and Sekou Toure's *L'Experience Guineene et l'Unite Africaine,* reveal this approach. They underestimated the neocolonial character of what had been achieved, and were simplistic in their understanding of the inherent constraints of this route to African unity. Later with the establishment of the Organization of African Unity (OAU), and the political paralysis which has dogged its path from the start, it became increasingly clear that the way to African unity had to be sought through other instrumentalities. None of the regional groupings that Africa has seen since the 1960s has made much headway, and even those like the East African Community which were put in place by the colonial power Britain have not stood the test of time.

The African Malaise and the Way Forward

Thirty years after the onset of the era of independence, it is clear that African states are economically unviable, politically fragile and inept, socially unintegrated and developmentally moribund. Autocratic rule, first by one-party states, and later military-bureaucratic dictatorships have silenced civil society, and shredded the moral fabric of African society. State revenue is treated as booty by the ruling groups. Whilst the African crisis has pushed the agenda for unity into the background, unity remains the only way forward to African development. Pan-Africanism is the only way to contain rampant ethnic fissures. With the completion of the independence process in South Africa through the dismantling of Apartheid and settler-colonial rule, I would argue that, the next area of serious contention, lies in the Afro-Arab borderlands.

In the Sudan and Mauritania, slavery of Africans continues. Arabisation processes and African denationalization is fomenting war in the whole region. The OAU is unable to deal with internal matters

86

affecting African states, because of its protocols. The war in the Sudan has dragged on intermittently since August 1955. Uganda is unable to bring its war to a close. Angola and Mozambique are emerging out of decades of fratricidal conflict. Somalia, Liberia and Sierra Leone are ruled by warlords. We have seen the cruel degeneracy of Mengistu's Ethiopia, Marcias Nguema's Equatorial Africa, Amin's Uganda, Bokassa's Central African Empire, Numeiri's Sudan, and Doe's Liberia. Babangida and now Abacha's Nigeria, Eyadema's deadening dictatorship in Togo, the long-lasting Mobutu in Zaire, the shambles and absurdities of mercenary-ravaged Comores and the atavistic barbarities of Rwanda and Burundi plague the African scene. Poverty, corruption, and mismanagement has brought African countries on their knees, and most states exist through the largesse of the metropolitan powers and donor agencies of the world. Through the global economic system, Africa has been saddled with a crushing debt-burden. The age of neocolonialism has reached maturity but conditions are likely to worsen, before they start getting better. For decades, state capitalism has been packaged and sold as socialism, and populist rhetoric used to camouflage socio-economic cleavages.

African advancement and the establishment of democratic practice requires the involvement of a literate mass society. This literate society cannot be developed on the basis of the borrowed colonial languages which serve the mimetic culture of the elite, and which dismiss by implication the viability of the history and culture of Africans. If mass society in Africa is to be empowered and creatively freed, this can only be achieved on the premise of African historico-cultural belongings, with selective borrowing and adaptations, which do not negate the cultural roots of people. But most of these cultures transcend existing colonially imposed borders, thus the argument leads directly to the need to slowly work against the impositions of these borders, and install institutions along Pan-Africanist lines which strengthen social intercourse amongst Africans.

Language: The Missing Link

Language is the axis of all cultures. It is in language that the total historical experience of all human groups are constructed and continuously transacted. The condition, structure and development of any given language reflects the historical record of the society or societies which use that language. Social and linguistic life, demographic transformations, technological innovations, the trajectory of economic history and cultural relations, can all be appreciated from linguistic history. Linguistics in a way offers Africa, with its relatively poor written historical legacy a significant source and facility for information and data on Africa's heritage.

All languages by their very nature have their audiences. These social catchment areas are the language-communities, which use in each instance a specific language. A multi-lingual person in effect, belongs to as many language-communities, as he or she is familiar with. Africans indeed constitute some of the most multi-lingual people on earth. Language-communities are socio-cultural entities structured in space and time. The measure of creativity is the extent to which people can reach new and innovative levels of thought-synthesis which permit interventions in reality. But thought itself is partly a function of linguistic insights and the ability to organize new ideas on the basis of commonly shared language symbols. This requires familiarity and command. It is therefore inconceivable to create and press the human genius into useful service in a language we can hardly use. In short, we create best in our home or first languages.

Languages are either purely oral, as is the case for preliterate peoples, or both spoken and written in the case of literate societies. Literacy opens up possibilities for increasing the fund of culture available to people. Whether spoken and/or written, languages are systems of symbols whose meanings are socially shared and constructed in a ceaselessly changing fashion. Languages bloom or perish in response to the historical affluence of the societies they socially define. As changing and open systems, they adapt and absorb new forms or terms as they evolve towards growth or extinction. If they grow, they increase in volume and differentiation. As they die they fail to keep abreast with new realities. Of course, the extinction or death of a language, does not in most instances mean the physical disappearance of the users. What it most often means is that, the users have been totally integrated into another cultural system; another language system. Languages, like the cultures they represent, mix. This has been the case from Adam, and will continue on a faster and wider scale as communication in the global village increases.

Most African societies have until the last century been preliterate. This is so inspite of the fact that, the first stages in the development of writing in the human experience appeared in Egypt around 4000 BC. There are parts of the Sahel and the Horn area of the continent where the tradition of writing independent of western European initiation, is of ancient ancestry. Because of the fact that most of Africa has until recent times been preliterate, the corpus of literature in African languages is spare and for the most part evangelical and Christian, and has come with the penetration of the west in Africa. Almost single-handedly, missionaries have been responsible for the rendering of African languages into written forms. The challenge has always been to provide Africans with the Bible in their own languages. While it was reasoned that this was the best way of reaching into the depths of the African mind, the extension of all reading in native tongues was never favourably considered, since, that would have stood in the way of the colonial endeavour.

An important point to be noted is the fact that, because African languages have been largely preliterate, and provide a poor fund for the African cultural heritage, they as living forms in everyday usage have become the living sources of the cultures and history of Africans. In their everyday, living and orally rendered forms, they bear the histories and collective consciousness of Africans as cultural products. They indeed define what is African in the human community as a distinct contributory source. In this sense, they are therefore undoubtedly critical for the maintenance of an African identity. But their importance is not based only on this consideration. Equally importantly, their prospective role in education, and the scientific and technological advancement of Africa, is in my view, one of the most pressing challenges facing Africans today. The fate of the resolution of this question, will decide whether Africa develops or not.

In the experience of the contemporary world, no society which is scientifically and technologically advancing, is achieving this on the basis of a language foreign to its peoples. This is a point which in my view has not been fully appreciated in Africa. Scientific concepts and the thought-processes of conceptualization itself are grounded in a socio-cultural matrix. This matrix is the totality of the reality in which a people live, both as a historically constructed cumulative cultural assemblage, and nature as socially perceived and collectively shared, in the understanding of a people through the agency of language. While reality is in its materiality a constant factor, no two languages as distinct cultural derivatives have identical representations. Translations are approximations seen from different language systems. But good translations, internally structurize and logically order the perceptions of reality based in different languages to the same end. Taking the argument into another direction, one would say that, in African education, to give mathematical or biological examples drawn from European realities to African students is to force the cultivation of mimicry and not creativity in the minds of such students. The function of education is not to put into place the conditions for cultural schizophrenia, rather, it is to provide the tools for people to relate and mould their cultures to suit human needs in the first instance in their own societies and their own realities.

In a recent argument presented to the UNESCO, I make the point that, few myths about African languages and cultures enjoy as much baseless but rampant recognition as the view that, Africa has literally thousands of languages. There is no doubt that the African continent fields a large number of languages. Most of them are closely related and have fairly high degrees of mutual intelligibility. Furthermore, Africa is a huge continent. Indeed, it is the second largest continent.

The above myth that Africa has a babel of languages; that it is impossible to move a few kilometres from one place to the next without coming into another language area was initiated during the colonial period. A number of reasons can be found to explain the origins of this illusion. For one thing, missionary linguists were fairly idiosyncratic in the way they developed orthographies and through such practices projected their own views in the creation of separate identities for people who were not really ethno-linguistically different.

The early western ethnographers and anthropologists were invariably keen to "discover their own tribes". Colonial administrators

90

were also quick in their effort to administratively divide areas up into manageable bits and pieces, which were then, often from above, vested with distinct identities. During the early decades of the colonial interlude, in many areas, in especially the acephalous societies, chiefs, warrant-chiefs, headmen and rulers were created where they did not exist, often with disastrous consequences, as was the case in Iboland. Such colonially induced structural infeudation and the emergence of myriad administrative units, with often different traditional authorities, created polities which did not exist before the colonial era. With remuneration under the colonial dispensation for such traditional authorities, the colonially created polities tended to guard their new found identities and quickly internalized new or revised mythologies of ethnic differentiation.

Colonialism created a new Africa, a new Africa in which Africans were given new identities by colonial overlords. There was no grand design behind this, except in as far as such socio-structural ordering was not permitted to contradict the intentions and activities of individual colonial authorities, or the coexistential protocols reached between the imperial powers. These latter were largely adopted and revised in stages from the mid-1880s to 1918. By the 1920s, the colonially sponsored designations as they have been handed down and inherited to the present period were more or less in place. The only area of Africa where significant revisions have in recent decades been made has been French West Africa at the beginning of the 1960s. Then, Charles De Gaulle, under increasing pressure to decolonize French colonial Africa, hurriedly chopped up the area into little fragments.

Through a convergence of the effects of missionary linguistics, colonial anthropology and administrative practice, dialects were frequently given the status of languages. With little or no attempts at standardization, these dialects over time acquired de facto regard as separate languages.

Figures provided by the 1980 Lome Seminar on the *Problems of Language Planning in A Bi- or Multilingual Context* on the numbers of African languages, indicated a range according to different criteria, of estimates from about 1250 to 2100. In his recent study *Africa's*

Choices: After Thirty Years of the World Bank, Michael Barratt Brown boldly repeats this myth (27). By Fafunwa's account, 120 clusters have been identified. 85% of the languages are concentrated in the "fragmentation belt" which covers the latitudinal space of the area as far north as the Senegambia basin, to Ethiopia, and down to Northern Tanzania. 120 clusters have been identified. In my estimation the figure is actually very much lower. It has been estimated that 75% of the languages in the "fragmentation belt" belong to the two groups of Hamito/Semitic/Afro-Asiatic and the Niger Congo. Actually Afro-Asiatic is generic to Hamito/Semitic. In any case the Meinhofian Hamitic theory enjoys little currency today. Furthermore, whether the Niger Congo phylum is an offshoot of Proto-Afro-Asiatic or more immediately related to Chadic is evidentially contestable. Fafunwa has reproduced a UNESCO table on, *Languages Used Across National Boundaries* which is rather poor (28). For example, if Setswana is understood in its narrow sense, it features in Namibia, Botswana and South Africa, not two countries as the UNESCO table suggests. In a wider and more significant sense Setswana is part of the wider Sotho-Tswana cluster which includes Lozi in Barotseland. Somali is spoken in five countries but does not appear on the table. Evidence indeed suggests that well over 90 percent of African languages are spoken across borders.

Another example would be that if Luo is used as a restricted descriptive category it covers parts of three countries (Kenya, Uganda and Tanzania). In generic usage, in the sense in which it has been used by Crazzollara or Okot Bitek, its coverage will include in geographical scope an area as wide as parts of the Sudan, Ethiopia, Uganda, Kenya, and Tanzania. In either case it cannot be two as the table shows. Proximate and mutually intelligible dialects of the Luo language in Eastern Africa for example are referred to under various designations as Jur (Sudan), Anyuak (Sudan and Ethiopia), Shilluk (Sudan and Ethiopia), Acholi (Sudan and Uganda), Langi (Uganda), Alur (Uganda), Chopadholla (Uganda) and Luo (Uganda, Kenya, Tanzania). Kikuyu, Embu, Meru, Akamba in Kenya are closely related dialects. The Bari-speaking people in the Sudan have been "analytically chopped up" into Mondari, Bari, Nyangbara, Fajelu,

Kakwa (Uganda, Sudan, Zaire), and Kuku (Uganda and Sudan). Kipsigi, Nandi, Pokot, Elgeyo Marakwet are not separate languages, but rather dialects of Kalengin. In Ghana, the Akan have been in the anthropological literature referred to as Ashanti, Fanti, Agona, Kwahu, Akim, Akuapim, Nzema, and even sub-units of these like Ahanta, Gomua, Edina etc. The Ewe-speaking people can be found in communities all along the West African Coast from Ghana through Togo, Benin and to the Nigerian border area. In East Africa, the Teso, Kumam, Karamojong, Dodos, Jie, Turkana, Toposa, Donyiro collectively cover areas in Kenya, Uganda and the Sudan. The Nguni are found in Tanzania where they closely relate ethnolinguistically to the Nyamwezi, they are also located in Malawi, in Mozambique they are identified as the Shangaan, Swaziland as Swati, Kangwane in northern Natal/Zululand, Zulu in South Africa, Xhosa in South Africa, Ndebele in South Africa and Matabeleland in Zimbabwe. The Sotho-Tswana cluster is to be found as Tswana in Namibia, Tswana in Botswana, Lozi in Barotseland/Zambia, Sotho in Lesotho, and Pedi in South Africa. Again in East Africa, the Inter-lacustrine Bantu have a high degree of mutual intelligibility. They include the Nyoro, Toro, Haya, Ganda, Ankole, Rwanda. Borana and Oromo are literally the same. Maasai and Samburu are equally close. Fulful, Fulbe, Fulde, Fulani, Fula, Peul, Pula, Tuculor is spoken in 13 countries captured by the area within Senegambia, Darfur and the Northern Cameroon. It has about 40-50 million speakers. The Hausa based mainly in the Cameroon, Niger and Nigeria also number about 50 million. The Oromo speakers in mainly Ethiopia, and Kenya are a little less than the Hausa speaking peoples. In the two countries Benin and Nigeria, Yoruba is spoken by between 30-40 million people. Swahili is a shared language in Eastern and large parts of Central Africa. In short, the myth of the African Tower of the Babel has weak scientific foundations. The whole area of work needs to be revisited, with a view to updating and improving on the monumental work of Joseph Greenberg and his scholastic progeny.

If the success of African education and emancipation, development and unity depends on the usage of African languages, this however, cannot be done in an haphazard manner. There is firstly, the need for a revision of the ethnolinguistic map of Africa which would reflect more accurately the distribution of language clusters on the continent, based on accurate measurement of degrees on mutual intelligibility. This must be done in a comprehensive fashion. It will need to involve linguists, anthropologists, sociologists and historians. Clusters would need to be determined in a way that in effect tolerate dialectal differences without such differences inhibiting or creating divergencies in meaning.

Furthermore, there is also the need for the standardisation of orthographies within clusters. This will allow over time the dialects to grow into each other, and permit the sharing of an increased common social space. As I have indicated above, a great deal of these orthographical differences have emerged on account of the different backgrounds of the missionaries and early linguists who worked with African languages. It is arguable that indeed, to some extent, the proliferation and ethnification of cultural sub-sets in Africa has been facilitated by the distinctive localization and orthographic restrictions which these different orthographies have projected in the identification of language communities. Tribes were invented. This has resulted in "identities" being foisted on groups which did not previously exist.

If African languages are reclassified on the basis of degrees of mutual intelligibility, it will be possible to create demographic matrices for large literary communities which with economies of scale will be rational as markets for literature and other media forms. There is little doubt that in economic terms such structural linguistic aggregation, clustering and the standardization of proximate versions within clusters of high mutual intelligibility will decisively transform publishing in these languages into profitable business. It is also likely to require and promote greater cooperation between African states, which in turn will minimize ethnically mobilized conflict. It will enhance the process of scientific and technological knowledge transfer, and facilitate the empowerment of mass society in Africa. It should also to be pointed out that as a scientific endeavour in its own right, it is work which needs to be done. The issue of developing and using indigenous languages for mass education and the cultivation of a literate mass culture is a pressing problem in contemporary Africa.

The clustering and standardization if orthographies within clusters will create a cultural institutional base for the development of African unity at the mass level. It will provide the cultural tools for the masses to confront and negate the impact of imperialism, a task which the elite, by its very coopted character is incapable of. It will diminish the effects of the neocolonial borders and provide a developmental grid for African cultures as a basis for the advancement of African society.

Notes.

1. Hans Kohn and Wallace Sokolsky. *African Nationalism in the Twentieth Century*. Princeton. 1965. p.84.

2. Barbara Ward. *Nationalism and Ideology*. London. 1967. p.48.

3. Elliot Skinner. "The Dialectic between Diasporas and Homelands". In, *Joseph E. Harris (ed). Global Dimensions of the African Diaspora*. Washington. 1982. pp.17-18.

4. George Shepperson. "African Diaspora: Concept and Context". In, J.E. Harris. Ibid. pp.46-47.

5. Orunu Lara. "African Diaspora: Conceptual Framework. Problems and Methodological Approaches". In, J.E. Harris. p.57.

6. J.E. Harris. "Introduction". Ibid. p.6.

7. Tony Martin. "Garvey and Scattered Africa". In, J.E. Harris. Ibid. p.243.

8. W.E.B. Du Bois. *The Autobiography of W.E.B. Du Bois*. New York. 1968. W.E.B. Du Bois. *The World and Africa*. New York. 1947. Ras Makonnen. *Pan-Africanism from Within*. OUP. London. 1973. George Padmore. *Pan-Africanism or Communism*. London. 1956. Kwame Nkrumah. *I Speak of Freedom*. New York. 1961. K. Nkrumah. *Africa Must Unite*. New York. 1963. K. Nkrumah. *Ghana. An Autobiography*. Edinburgh. 1956.

9. Philippe Decraene. *Le Panafricanisme*. Presses Universitaires de France. Paris. 1961. J.R. Hooker. Henry Sylvester Williams. *Imperial Pan-Africanist*. London. 1975. E.D. Cronon. *Black Moses. The Story of Marcus Garvey*. Madison. 1955. Alex Quaison-Sackey. *Africa Unbound*. New York. 1963. Immanuel Geiss. *The Pan-African Movement*. London. 1974. Colin Legum. *The Roots of Pan-Africanism*. London. 1961.

10. J.R. Hooker. Ibid. pp.31-32.

11. Kwame Anthony Appiah. *In My Father's House*. Methuen. London. 1991. p.69

12. Francis Broderick. "German Influence on the Scholarship of W.E.B. Du Bois". *Phylon 11. Winter 1958*. pp.367-371.

13. W.E.B. Du Bois. "The Conservation of Races". In, Philip S. Foner (ed). *W.E.B. Du Bois Speaks*. New York. 1986. p.75.

14. H.E. Barnes. "Social Thought in Early Modern Times". In, H.E. Barnes (ed). *An Introduction to The History of Sociology*. Chicago. 1966. pp.58-59.

15. W.E.B. Du Bois. *Dusk of Dawn*. p.626. Quoted here from *Paul Gilroy. The Black Atlantic*. Cambridge; Mass. 1993. p.134. That Du Bois intellectually and psychologically survived the Prussian chauvinist atmosphere of late 19th century Berlin is in itself remarkable. "The great" Von Treitschke's anthropogeography is noteworthy. In one of his lectures he suggested that, "... what example of artistic greatness has proceeded from the magnificent Alpine countries? Relatively very little. Walther von der Vogelweide, if he really came thence, would be the only great poet that the Tyrol has brought forth; and even Switzerland has only lately produced a true poet in Gottfried Keller. It has always been the case that a country of lofty mountains has only by way of exception been the seat of higher culture. There simple conditions exist, heroic jäger-natures, men for the most part sturdy and well built, but also of limited outlook. On the contrary, countries with mountains of moderate height, like the charming valleys of Suabia and Franconia and the friendly chains of green heights of Thuringia, have produced a multitude of poets and artists". *(Selections from Treitschke's Lectures on Politics. London, 1914. Translated by Adam L. Gowans.* p.54.) His strongly imperialist ideas are also remarkable. He asserts that, "the English are the most fortunate. The population of this little island has thrown out so many shoots that there are already at the present time more than a hundred millions of people of English descent. In this fact alone is the importance of colonies revealed. A nation which seeks to acquire new realms of exploitation, in order to be able to support its growing population, shows the courage of its confidence in God. The contemptuous way in which these deeply serious things are discussed at the present time is simply appalling. People sing a new song to the old tune: 'Be smaller, fatherland of mine!' That is simply turning the world upside-down. We wish and ought to take our share in the domination of the world by the white race". Ibid. p.55.

16. James J. Cooke. *New French Imperialism. The Third Republic and Colonial Expansion*. Newton Abbot and Hamden.. 1973. p.21.

17. Helmuth Stoecker (ed). *German Imperialism in Africa*. Berlin. 1986. pp.209-210.

18. Ibid.

19. Emile Boonzaier." 'Race' and the Race Paradigm". In, *E. Boonzaier and J. Sharp (ed). South African Keywords. The Uses and Abuses of Political Concepts*. Cape Town. 1988. p.61.

20. H. Stoecker. Op cit. p.210.

21. W.E.B. Du Bois. "Credo". In, Philip Foner (ed). Ibid. p.142.

22. Quoted here from Paul Gilroy. Op cit. p.111.

23. August Meier. *Negro Thought in America. 1880-1915*. 1978 edition. University of Michigan Press. Ann Arbor. pp. 194-195.

24. K.A. Appiah. Op cit. p.64.

25. K.K. Prah. "Pan-Africanism Revisited". (Mimeo). Kampala. 1994.

26. See, Ras Makonnen. *Pan-Africanism from Within*. OUP. London. 1973. p.112.

27. M. Barratt Brown. *Africa's Choices. Thirty Years of the World Bank*. Harmondsworth. 1995. p.122.

28. Babatunde A. Fafunwa. "Using National Languages in Education: A Challenge to African Educators". In, *African Thoughts on the Prospects of Education for All. Selections from Papers Commissioned for the Regional Consultation on Education for All*. Dakar. 27th-30th November 1989. p.99 and p.102.

Joseph Oduho - An African Patriot.

Cape Town
February 12, 1995

Last week, I received a letter from a former student, Robin Ben Oduho, a Sudanese I taught in the University of Juba over twelve years ago. The last few times I met him in 1983, he was putting plans in place to continue his studies. He ended up in the African nationalist resistance in the Sudan, as part of the Sudan Peoples Liberation Army (SPLA). From this organization, he is today estranged and disappointed, by the way the SPLA under Dr. John Garang has conducted itself and fared.

Robin Ben Oduho's disillusionment is shared by a wide variety of other intellectuals who joined the SPLA from the early beginnings in 1983. Complaints about the lack of democratic decision-making and the cult of personality has dogged the path of the SPLA since 1985, and has become the source of internal bloodletting and haemorrhage, which has gone on to the extent that today, the African national liberation movement in the Sudan is as splintered, as it was at the closing stages of the first civil war (1955-1972). The tragedy of the masses, the ultimate victims of the conflict is increased by the disputed leadership and elusive unity within the African nationalist movement.

The last time I saw Robin Ben Oduho, I had contacted him in Juba, to request him to take a message to his uncle Joseph Haworu Oduho in Torit District. The message which had been passed to me by our common friend Sirr Anai Keleuljang was that, there was a warrant for the arrest of "Uncle Joe". If he came back to Juba from his home district, he would be picked up by the Security Police of the regime. Oduho never came back to Juba again. He became part of and a leading member of the SPLA, he was imprisoned by the SPLA, released and restored, but not to his deserving position of influence. He was murdered by SPLA forces on the 24th of March 1993, while

98

on a mission to help reconcile rival factions of the movement in the Southern Sudan.

Robin Ben Oduho took the message to his uncle with Uncle Joe's own son Kizito who also subsequently joined the war and lost his life a few years ago. Of his generation, in the university, Kizito was the golden boy, I remember him as a bright, cheerful, alert and courageous personality, this latter quality he shared with his father.

Robin Ben Oduho's letter is particularly painful because it gives an account of how Joseph Oduho died in the hands of the same interests for whose freedom he had all his life struggled. Oduho is one of the great names of the African revolution this century. His whole life has been in the struggle and died (like his own child) in the struggle. His name and memory together with others will undoubtedly go down in the annals of the history of the African freedom struggle, to be remembered and cherished as an example of commitment to the cause of African emancipation for the coming generations.

In his own words, in a document passed on to me in Addis Ababa in 1987, he writes that, in the events following the Torit Mutiny of the 17th of August 1955, which marked the commencement of the first civil war;

> ...the Sudanese Arabs accused Southern Sudanese intelligentsia for the breakout of the revolt. I was consequently one of the many suspected, arrested and falsely charged for the murder of an Arab teacher in my school. I was tried and convicted and sentenced to death on November the 15th 1955. I was eventually acquitted on appeal on the first of January 1956. It is this event (the Mutiny and its aftermath) -- the slave trade apart -- which had embittered South Sudan against the Arab North. Many were given mock trials and executed. It was during those days of tribulations that I resolved to fight for the freedom of South Sudan should I escape execution.

This is the man who in December 1960 had fled the country with other famous leaders like, Ferdinand Adiang, Mbali Yango, Nathaniel Oyet, Saturnino Lohure, Pancrasio Ochieng and William Deng, in the face of a threat of arrest by the Arabist Sudanese authorities. Oduho became the first president of the first African freedom movement for the Sudan in the post-colonial period called, the Sudan African Closed Districts National Union (SACDNU), which for reason of "the awkwardness of its initials" was later changed to SANU or Sudan African National Union. He was instrumental in the organization of the Anya-Nya, the armed wing of the movement.

After the Addis Ababa Agreement of 1972, Oduho served as Minister, in the Southern Regional Government. Right from the beginning of this period, he was unhappy with the direction events took. He was arrested in 1976 and released the following year. As the Numeiri regime proceeded to dismantle the Addis Ababa Agreement piece by piece and decreed the division of the South the embers of war were rekindled. Oduho was "back into the bush".

I came to know Joseph Oduho well in the Sudan. We spent many good hours together talking about the African struggle at home and in the diaspora, but mainly about the Sudanese struggle. Oduho was a man who could not bear hypocrites and liars. He was always forthright and fearless both in word and deed. He never minced words. In his demeanour, Oduho was always a man at ease with himself. He was self-confident and was self-assured of the justness of the cause for which he paid the ultimate price.

Those who killed Oduho will bear the unmitigated judgement of history. Nobody, looking at the life of Oduho, can doubt where he stood in the broad sweep of events. I last spoke to him, on a long distance phone call (Nairobi to Cape Town) he made to me, coincidentally, at a time when the Anglican Archbishop of the Southern Sudan was with a delegation visiting Cape Town for a conference and were in fact having lunch in my house. I never either saw or spoke to him again. Within six weeks of our last conversation, he was dead, murdered by SPLA forces under the command of Cdr. Kuol Manyang Juuk.

It is important for the emerging youth in Africa never to forget Joseph Oduho and others like Benjamin Bol Akok, Martin Majier and Joe Malath excellent cadres who have been lost through internecine turmoil. If the Sudan African struggle is to move forward successfully, we need to find a united basis of the struggle. Democratic practice must rule all areas of activity.

Deep down, I know that the emancipation of the African people in the Sudan, for which Oduho lived and died will in the end triumph. As the saying goes; "no one can stop the rain".

The Tripoli Initiative and the Tasks of the Pan-African Movement Today.

Cape Town.
March 1996.

Dear Tajudeen,

It was good meeting you in Manchester. It was very useful that Manchester 1995 happened and provided a platform for interested parties to take stock of the record, and reflect on future prospects. The organizers deserve unreserved credit for the undertaking.

It was largely an academic meeting, with a fractional activist representation. However, unfortunately, very few of the presenters had written papers we could share. I only discovered late, that there were in fact three celebrations of the 50th anniversary taking place at the same time, and that there had been considerable organizational rivalry and politicking in the events leading to our meeting. These rivalries obviously represented differences in the constituency of Pan-Africanists and students of Pan-Africanism. What all this meant of course was that, we could not have the optimum level of interaction of "kindred souls" and proximate minds, as one would have wished.

There was a near absence of people from the Francophone and Lusophone corners of Africa and the diaspora. I particularly missed talking to Clarke and Curruthers who were at one of the other meetings. It was a memorable meeting. I had not seen Sivanandan, Stella Dadzie, Colin Prescod, Kofi Klu, Immanuel Geiss, and Nabudere for some time, so it was a chance to review the past.

Hearing the thorough Marable, charged Alkalimat, the paced Carew, rational Ransby, sedately poetic Robinson, and trenchant Lewis gave me something to remember. Jules- Rossette was languid, learned and lyrical, I found her artistry affecting, but her contribution was more aesthetically pleasing than analytically convincing. Her contribution was however, the only significant attempt at the meeting to bring into focus, "francophone responses to Pan-Africanism". Nabudere's contribution pointed out the need to transcend states to "people", as the ultimate units of the Pan-African project. While I had some doubts about Marable's specific reading of the Post-Cold war scenario, the general outline of his contention that, "Pan-Africanism as a political vision must be reframed to address the new and changing ethnic, class and social realities of the 21st century" was useful and convincing. Lisa Aubrey's presentation was couched in the latter mould. J.K. Adjaye's contribution was a painstaking effort but lacked philosophical or methodological consistency. It was unconsciously eclectic; a position involuntarily arrived at, and with little display of awareness of the implications or philosophical underpinnings of the position. Alkalimat's new class of permanently unemployed, forced out of the capitalist social contract, captured the economic essence of the plight of the African-American lower classes in the contemporary US. It is corroborated by what the Guinean historian Boubacar Barry said recently to me in his description of the situation of the North American diaspora. He said "the failure of the American system is illustrated by the existence of countless examples of three generations of African-Americans living on the dole". The American underclass is eminently African-American. They over-populate both the dole queues and the prisons.

Babatunde's argument was inspired and vigorously presented, but logically disjointed and truncated. Kofi Klu, who I met after 20 years, has maintained the pulsating activist commitment he had as a teenager under the guardianship of Wentum Kitcher. His activist fervour is reassuring but he has embraced what appears to me to be the neo-mystical variety of North American Afrocentricism and the MAAT ideology. In as far as Afrocentricism seeks to situate the African at the centre of his or her view of society and the world (like all others do), I have no problem with it. But when, in the language of J. H. Clarke it begins to scale the heights of mysticism to "reveal and reaffirm the Way of Maat (Wat-n-Maat)", or as Maulana Karenga suggests, "a well-defined path and pattern of human life which offers an ascendant paradigm, not only for ourselves as Africans, but for History and Humanity in the true Spirit of our Kemetic Ancestors, the Sun People, who were truly the Light and Warmth of the World", although, I share the sentiment which inspires this position, I part company with the intellectual foundations of such neo-mysticism.

Wolf-Peter Martin provided us with a stimulating account of the COMINTERN's relationship with the International Negro Workers Conference in Hamburg (1930). The meeting was a bit harsh in its reception of Immanuel Geiss's argument. His criticism of the post-colonial Pan-African record was uncomplimentary but I would suggest not misplaced.

Meeting the Makonnen children from all corners was wonderful and David Du Bois gave the meeting further historical and familial investiture. The three Mancunians who variously recollected to us, their experience of the 1945 meeting embodied more than half a century of the African and Afro-Caribbean experience in Britain. The meeting had its high and low points; some seriousness, occasional raucousness, calculated buffoonery and incidental absurdities. Nana Ohene Darko and Prince Frederick Von Saxe-Lakenberg were differently but equally surreal.

You did mention the fact that, you were from Manchester going on to Washington to witness "the million man march" of "the Nation of Islam". The event has since then generated a lot of print, approval and invective. I admire and respect the fact that, they have succeeded to engage the grassroots of African-America so effectively, but for me given the philosophically reactionary and strategically narrow base of Farrakhan's views, I have difficulty with "the Nation of Islam". One would however be sectarian and elitist to suggest that they should be shunned. They are too important and too significant to be treated or regarded lightly. They should be engaged but not courted, wooed but not married. The success of this particular movement in fact shows the intellectual and organizational bankruptcy of other ideological tendencies within the African-American community. It demonstrates the contemporary barrenness and desertification of the landscape of ideas for African-American advancement. It reveals the desperate straits and leadership vacuum which faces the African freedom movement in the United States. Since the demise of leaders like Du Bois, Robeson, King and Malcolm X, no leader has captured the imagination with any degree of convincing firmness or compelling vision. Andrew Young became too quickly establishmentarian. Abernathy never got started, and can be said in later years to have become a Judas Iscariot of King's memory. Jesse Jackson tried to fill the place of King, but beyond the Rainbow Coalition and two doomed attempts at the presidential stakes he has fallen to the level of a talk-show host. If, this is where the leadership of the masses of African-America are today, there is obviously need for serious intellectual and organizational work facing the emergent generation of African-Americans.

In Kampala I raised the question of the right to citizenship on demand in Africa, by the diaspora, I went back to it again in Manchester. Indeed, it is a theme which has been present in Pan-Africanist ideology since the late 18th and early 19th centuries. Throughout the 19th century, colonization and Back to Africa movements have been principal and abiding issues in the concerns of Pan-Africanists. They are even expressed in the lyrics of the spirituals. We all know that the overwhelming majority of the diaspora have no wish to return to the continent. But the right to return is the right of the African nation, it is their right. It is the right of overseas Africans if ever there was one. It is the sort of policy which will give meaning to African unity.

Every time we affirm the diasporal link, we unite Africans and also transcend continentalism in the process. But of course, this is all only of use if it ultimately serves the wider interests of humanity as a whole. Otherwise it becomes a reactionary position prey to bigoted flag-waving and jingoism.

The relevance of alliances and cooperative relations with democratic movements and emancipatory processes worldwide must not be lost on us. To share ideas with such movements serves humanity, enriches our understanding and helps inform practice better. European unity, which is slowly evolving before us, will unite and strengthen the cultural heritage of Europe, but more importantly, it will enable the sharing of such institutions by mass society in Europe. The advancement of Arab unity is a challenge which can only grow with time and pursuit. Pan-Africanism will need to correspond with such endeavours. They represent similar conjunctures in the democratic process as a global phenomenon.

Bernie Grant was farcical on the Sudan and I had great difficulty with his confused popery. For a British parliamentary of African descent not to know that there is African slavery by Arabs in the Sudan is inexcusable. Recently I picked up an article by Brian Eads, in the *Readers Digest* (March 1996, pp-31-32), part of which I want to share with you.

> Slavery has returned in Sudan, Africa's largest country. Behind the cloak of a brutal civil war, tens of thousands of people have been abducted from their homes and sold like chattel, in the same way as Abuk was last March. Some are bought by individuals to serve as field workers, household servants or concubines. Others, confined in camps, work on government farms or are leased to large landowners. There are frequent and consistent reports that slaves are being exported to Libya and countries on the Persian Gulf.

Some people draw attention to tensions between people of African descent in the diaspora; West Indians and North Americans in the US, North Americans and Africans in the US, West Indians and continental Africans in the UK and France, colour and status gradations in the US, Brazil and the West Indies, and the contradictions and absurdities of coloureds and blacks in South Africa. To this can be added fratricidal barbarities like we have seen in recent years in Somalia, and Rwanda 1994 (which indeed broke out last year while we were next door in Kampala for the 7th PAC).

In our closing session, I had a quiet conversation with David Du Bois. It concerned his continentalist notions of Pan-Africanism. He asked, if I do not consider Arabic to be an African language. I told him, I think it is spoken by many Africans especially in the northern areas of the continent but that does not make it an African language. English and French are spoken by many more Africans but that does not make them African languages. The problem with that part of Africa is not the mere usage of Arabic or varieties like Juba-Arabic, rather it is Arabisation. It is a process with a long history. It means the replacement of African cultural habits by purely Arab customs. Its fiercest flash point is in the present-day Sudan and other areas in the Afro-Arabs borderlands. Till today, the Berbers are fighting for language and cultural rights in the Mahgreb. The Nubians in Egypt are culturally beginning to stir. I remember the Sudanese archaeologist Ali Osman Mohammed Salih telling me in Bielefeld last year that the fundamentalist regime inspired by the fanatical *eminence grise* Hassan el Turabi has often placed obstacles in the way of his work on pre-islamic history and archaeology, lest it should overshadow the much younger Islamic experience.

Islam is in West Africa a millennium old, it constitutes an enriching heritage in West African culture. But West Africans have so far largely maintained the overwhelmingly African character of their cultural life. Moslems are to be found throughout Central Asia, the Philippines, Indonesia, Malaysia, Pakistan, Bangladesh, Iran and parts of China, but they hardly in any of the above mentioned instances regard themselves as Arabs on that account. Arabisation has for centuries not succeeded in Ethiopia or Somalia, and contrary to much consternation and fear, some years ago, when the Eritreans depended on the Arab States for support in the war against Selassie's regime and the successor Mengistu government, Eritrea has chosen the direction of its own cultures.

Tajudeen, the time has come for us to bury continentalism. If, only all people living on the African continent are Africans, our historical and cultural links across the Atlantic as a primary Pan-African connection becomes irrational. If we say our link is with the diaspora, we mean that we share a heritage in both historical and cultural senses (although the cultural bonds are becoming increasingly tenuous and need to be strengthened), with Africans from the continent taken forcibly across oceans and land masses over centuries. The intellectual and political process of African freedom on the continent has been inextricably bound with the diaspora.

It is of course historically enlightening to recall that for centuries before West Europeans took Africans into slavery in the Western hemisphere, Arabs had been busy at it. Unfortunately, to the present day Arab slavery continues. I am unable to understand Africans who want to wish this reality away, by playing the proverbial ostrich, putting their heads and senses into the sand and pretending to themselves that the reality somehow ceases to exist. Louis Farrakhan and Kwame Toure are both victims of this syndrome. I make this point without prejudice to the significant, but not faultless, contributions they have variously made to the movement for the emancipation of people of African descent. The democratic movement in the search for Arab unity does not lie in the corridors of power in the Arab world or the luxurious tents of Arab sheiks. It is not centred in governments and state structures. Such movements in the Arab states are outside the courtship of the zealotry and "modern prophetism" of the Khaddafi regime. They rest in the mass movements of the Arab world, the real social base of the democratic movement.

Col. Khaddafi may be renowned for claims of championship of the Arab nation and its unity, but certainly not the unity of the African nation. There are those who argue that there is, nothing like the African nation in-the-making or for the future, but that there is an Arab nation. Africa for them is like Metternich said of Italy before its consolidation, "simply geography"; only those on the African continent are Africans, but all of them are (such minds would argue) including even those who although born and bred on the continent, do not regard themselves as Africans, are Africans. Such argumentational formulation leads to the point, that therefore, the diaspora has at best a tenuous linkage with those on the continent. Furthermore, pursuing the logic of the assumption, Lybia and Tunisia are more African that Afro-Brazilians, West Indians, Guyanese or Afro-Americans. The absurdities pile up! The argument leads elsewhere; while allegiance to the Arab League represents inclusion in the Arab nation, the Organization of African Unity is a regional body, like the Organization of American States, it does not define the idea of the African nation. The pitfalls of continentalism are numerous. B.F. Bankie shares my strictures in this respect. It is an argument we reject. The OAU can and must remain a geographical grouping, but we need a body which defines us historically and culturally (not primarily on the basis of colour), a structure which links Africans to the diaspora, and which articulates its *raison d'etre* on the basis of the emancipation principle, and as part of general humanity.

We will not find this by submitting ourselves to the largesse of the Khaddafi regime. If we make the mistake of accepting Khaddafi's offer of hosting the next PAC, we will be submitting a vital institution for African emancipation and national unity to interests more immediately faithfully to the Arab League. I do not think this should happen. We should not play into the hands of groups whose primary focus is not African unity but Arab unity. If we do not have means we should wait until we can find the means from our own constituency. That way our autonomy and independence in decision-making in African affairs is better guaranteed.

Indeed, Tajudeen I hasten to add that this is also true with respect to other states on the continent. I do not think there is a single government on the continent today which for one reason or the other can serve as father or if you prefer godfather of the Pan-Africanist tendency in African nationalism. The states themselves are tragic creatures of neo-colonialism, they were at birth baptized by the departing colonial overlords as "nation-states" and set on the route to "nation-building". This latter has hardly happened and not likely to happen. African states would want to sponsor the Pan-African movement in order to direct and exploit it, for their own narrow intentions; for flag, anthem and the dominant elite.

The notion of the African nation, negates neo-colonial or "balkanized" nationhood. It denies the contention that African countries are nations. They are states created for purposes of maintaining imperialist domination through the rule of small-holders and military-bureaucratic elites. The dominant classes in these states are indiscriminately beholden to the culture of the west, and although they may rhetorically champion the cause of the wretched of the earth, their social and economic interests do not lie with the cultural and social empowerment of the deprived classes on the African continent and the diaspora, but with themselves in junior partnership with their neo-colonial masters.

Digesting Manchester 1995

Response to the Draft Document; Principles Agreed Upon at the 50th Anniversary of the Pan-African Congress in Manchester. 13-15, October 1995.

Cape Town
24 July 1996

Dear Barbara,

I was very happy to receive your letter yesterday, which attached the document, *Principles Agreed Upon At the 50th Anniversary of the Pan-African Congress in Manchester, Held Oct. 13-15, 1995, Manchester Town Hall.* Well done.

I hope you did receive my earlier letter to you. I recall with fond memories our conversation during our early afternoon walk from the Dominion Hotel to the Manchester Town Hall and the subsequent drink we had with Abdul Alkalimat in that old English pub talking about jazz and all that.

Your draft document brilliantly captures most of the key issues that attention needs to be drawn to, in a document like this. And to have been able to pack all that into one page is a considerable achievement. There is also a compacted succinctness and lucidity in your catalogue of points.

There are, however, a few points I would want to raise or react to with respect to the document. These points relate more to what is not said, than what is said. And in this respect, I may be under-reading, or over-reading you. All the same, I think for purposes of discourse and debate within our Movement, it is important for me to set out my ideas in black and white.

I like and agree with your point that if the Pan-Africanist Movement is to go forward into the next century and millennium with a message and a programme which is capable of meeting the challenges of the future, it would need to clearly make a break from biologically-based rationalizations of its theory and agenda. The way I put it is that we must go beyond the colour line.

Indeed, you may recall that was the point I made in my presentation to the meeting. But then when we say, as you say, that we should "come together in support of the political, economic and strategic unity of Africa and the African Diaspora", how and on what basis is this to be conceived and achieved? Colour is obviously an inappropriate and bankrupt basis to advance this point, and therefore, the only realistic basis for cogently arguing this objective is to premise the position on history and culture underpinned by democratic and emancipatory principles. The fact that people of African descent, who happen to be largely black in the contemporary world, are substantially the wretched of the earth, makes the process of liberation and empowerment, part of the general universal movement for freedom and emancipation. Whichever, and in whatever way, people of African descent democratically and humanely struggle for economic and social upliftment flows directly into the progress of humanity as a whole for freedom and self-assertiveness, over the existential conditions of their lives.

I say these things because without clarity on these matters some of these points may read rather platitudinous and cliched. They may indeed ring hollow and slogan-like if such points are inadequately structured and argumentatively rationalized. Obviously the emancipation and freedom of people of African descent, if it is democratically pursued, cannot run counter to the freedom of any other people. This is something we need to guard against, so that, we do not fall into the trap of chauvinists and xenophobes.

My other issue of concern with the document relates to the reference to "various forms of narrow cultural nationalism". I think that, taken at face value, this point can easily and with relevance stand as it is, but, it can also become ammunition in the hands of people who, on the basis of a blanket aversion to "nationalism", are unable to see its relevance under specific historical and cultural conditions.

Not all nationalism, under all conditions, is politically unprogressive and negative. I dare say even for Marxists, nationalism or nationalistic

111

programmes can, under specific historical conditions, constitute necessary prerequisites for the advancement and the emancipation of people who have been for long culturally and politically de-nationalized. There is enough evidence of numerous voices in the past and the present, who have articulated the misery and oppression suffered culturally, by colonized people throughout the world.

On the Continent, this particular experience is, in my estimation, responsible for the syndrome of cultural inferiority which pervades social life, particularly of the elite, and the capitulationist tendencies toward Western culture so prevalent in the social and cultural life of the people. It is, in many ways, the basis for the inertia inhibiting development on the African Continent. As a direct result of the colonial experience, African religious and ritual life was heathenized and paganized by the colonizers. The languages of the people were quietly, but implicitly, condemned to oblivion. To speak a European language is a passport to success in life. To speak your own language well and beautifully has, since the colonial encounter, lost its social relevance. Africans have been made to believe that, the way forward is to rival Shakespeare and Racine in their tongues. As I say in my study on J.E.J. Capitein, 1717-1747, today there are many Africans who would code switch in everyday discourse, believing quietly that by interjecting and interspersing their language with Anglicisms and Gallicisms, their discourse acquires polished and sophisticated status. Nowhere on the African Continent are African languages spoken with the verve, vibrancy and confidence which provides pride and thrust towards social, economic, and cultural advancement. This argument has, in various ways, been expressed by thinkers as diverse as Fanon, Kobina Sekyi, Casely Hayford, and Kenyatta. Without a cultural renaissance, the African masses cannot be empowered. As I often say, if we are waiting for the day when African people at the mass level, in their villages and urban shanties, will learn enough English, French, or Portuguese to create and innovate sufficiently to advance the quality of their lives, we would have to wait till "kingdom come". That day will never arrive.

What needs to be done is that the emancipation movement needs to be fleshed out and garbed with the cultural and historical belongings of the people. It is in that form that, the social and class struggles of mass society in Africa can be viably expressed. African advancement cannot go forward on the basis of Western culture. Certainly, elements of Western culture would need to be selectively adapted to suit African realities, in much the same way that other advancing formerly colonized peoples in Asia, particularly, are doing. The Asian Tigers, so much admired in the contemporary world, are not advancing on the basis of borrowed colonial languages or usages. Neither China nor Japan, with their giant leaps forward in technological advancement, are achieving this on the basis of the usage of Western languages. If we want to see the empowerment and democratization of the cultural and social lives of African people, we must understand that this can be achieved only on the basis of their languages and cultures. Far from constituting an unprogressive political or ideological position, cultural nationalism, expressed as a democratic and empowering instrument, is crucial for the forward march of African people.

I, however, hasten to add that, when I say this, I have no truck with varieties of nationalist programmes which articulate atavistic and mystical practices and which ring more of flat-footed populism. Neither am I supporting chauvinist or xenophobic expressions of nationalism, so common amongst right-wing and fascist ideologues.

I make the difference between the nationalism of the right and that of the left, between Hitler and Ho Chi Minh, between Peron and Mao Tse Tung. Nationalism for me is not essentially an ideology. It is a programme which, under certain historical conditions, is crucial as a step for the advancement of popular empowerment, emancipation and democracy. In our case, Africa can only advance on the basis of its own cultural and historical belongings, focused on the specificities, and directed towards African realities.

Deracializing Afrikanerdom

Revised Version of the Paper Presented to the Pre-Congress Colloquium of the 13th World Congress of Sociology. Bielefeld, Germany. July 15th-18th, 1994.

Introduction (1)

The cosmopolitanism of South Africa is inextricably linked with its ethnic mix. It is unrivalled in this respect on the African continent. No where else in Africa would you find this sort of diversity of sizeable communities from all corners of the world. They include apart from various groups of Europeans, Indians (2); and Chinese (3). Jews, Muslims, Hindus, Christians and other religionists who have historically been thrown together as compatriots. The cultural mix is tremendous and provides the basis of shared cultural space which will be the envy of most countries of the world.

This richness was fettered under apartheid and rather turned into caste-structures constructed around the notion of "basskap". Literally "boss-rule", but in this specific instance, Afrikaans-oriented white minority rule to preserve privilege. Until recently, the society had been organized in such a fashion that the lighter you were, the more you were socially endowed and rewarded. 70 percent of the national product went to the 16 percent white minority who own 87 percent of the land. The state machinery which enforced the system was draconian in its legislations and ruthless in the use of force to control the pressures for change. In all areas of social life including amenities, entertainment, housing, employment, education, health, immigration, population registration, taxation, territorial and residential distribution, a plethora of laws were instituted to ensure the separation of people with different skin colour. The most important laws created this century to organically prevent "racial mixing" were; the Immorality Act of 1927; the Population Registration Act of 1950; the Population Registration Amendment Act of 1962; the General Law Amendment Act of 1964; Population Registration Amendment Act of 1967; the Birth, Marriages and Deaths Registration Amendment Act of 1968;

the Population Registration Amendment Act of 1969 and 1970; the Prohibition of Mixed Marriages Act of 1949; the Immorality Amendment Act of 1950; and the Prohibition of Mixed Marriages Amendment Act of 1968 amongst others (4).

April 27th 1994 saw the formal end to the political power of the racist regime, which had directed affairs in South Africa since 1948. The National Party in South Africa was responsible for the institutionalization of Apartheid. However racism in South Africa predates Apartheid. The Apartheid system was the last and final stage of racial segregation and discrimination whose origins can be traced back to the early beginnings of settler-colonialism. Louw and Kendall indicate that the first racist law was passed in 1660. The first separate black school was started in 1663 and five years later in 1678 the Verenigde Oost-Indisch Compagnie (VOC) banned all inter-racial concubinage, "on pain of up to 3 years hard-labour imprisonment on Robben Island". Then in 1681, the VOC forbade whites to attend parties with slave (black) women. A special regulation was instituted forbidding marriage between whites and Khoikhoi. The first law which prohibited marriage between whites and blacks was established in 1685 (5). The earliest antecedent of the Pass System which was finally abolished in the 1980s was introduced in 1760 in the Cape. It required that slaves travelling between urban and rural areas carry passes from their masters. Later, the Pass Law System became a vagrancy arrangement serving in the enforcement of labour contracts which at the same time sanctioned and controlled movement. During the 19th century, British Pass Laws and the Masters and Servants Act insured the continuity of the system.

To maintain the claim to South Africa, for years the myth was advanced by the ideologues of white minority rule that "whites and blacks came to South Africa at about the same time". Another variant of this sort of myth-making was that, "the Bantu are not indigenous, they came in after the Dutch and British" (6). With respect to the Coloured community, in his *100 Questions about Coloured South Africans*, R.E. Van der Ross has indulged in similar myth-making which borrows directly from white Afrikaner imagery by suggesting that, "South African Coloured people and Blacks (Africans) only met

115

up with one another about 1770 on the Eastern frontier, near Port Elizabeth...". This sort of myth denies the African historical roots and component in the making of the Coloured community. Such falsifications attempt to implicitly deny the African character of the Khoi Khoi and the San and the African slaves, from both East and West Africa, brought into the Cape by the early Dutch settlers. Van der Ross's myth also fails to account for the emergence of other Coloured communities outside the Western Cape as the Trekboer moved inland.

In a letter which appeared in the Cape Argus of 2nd April 1997 written by Clement Kotze and entitled *Let's drop the exotica tags and just be South Africans,* the author wrote that,

> At the end of 1996, there was a lot of hype in the papers about the December 1st members reclaiming their roots. Some of them were photographed standing next to a tree stump, being sentimental about their slave ancestry. They also asserted that their attempts were to discover a coloured identity or solve the identity crisis affecting coloured people. This event reminded me of the time when I was a teacher in one of the Cape Flats schools recently. We sat one day in the staffroom and somehow talk drifted from misbehaviour of children to claims about ancestry. Talk of exotic origins ranged far and wide from Sweden to Switzerland, from England to Ireland. I was waiting to hear more when I was forced to inquire about our dark and tanned complexions. I received an equally exotic answer: "My dark complexion originates from Brazil," I was promptly told. To which I found myself automatically asking, "Not any local blood at all...?" The staffroom fell silent. You could even hear a piece of chalk drop. After a few pregnant moments of silence, one of my colleagues, seeing the "joke" in my question, chuckled uncomfortably and said "I suppose there is some..." The bell rang and saved me from awkward and concealed angry glances. To me, this occasion summed up a real problem that the coloured community have. And by now you should be able to guess what it is, the tendency to engage in ancestry escapism! I do not deny that the people in question have told a half-truth in some instances.

Kotze puts his finger directly on the problem. His diagnosis is faultless. He goes on to probe the whole issue even more testily, and we give him the length he deserves.

> ... let it not be an exercise in buffoonery, especially when lighthearted wishful thinking starts taking serious overtones. Your ancestry is right here, rediscover it and be proud of it..... A lot of coloureds are complaining in the now (in)famous words "We were not white enough in the past, nowadays we are not black enough!" The fact that I may have some Dutch "blood" is due to the worldwide process of colonisation. Mixing with the colonised was always a result of colonisation. Anyone who holds the fact that we are "mixed" against us is indeed holding the natural process of world history against us. In any case, show me any people on earth that are not mixed - I will show you a Martian.

This is actually very clear and substantial thinking. Kotze has evidently given serious and scorching thought to the whole issue. One of his parting shots was that,

> There are still a few Khoi-San left. Perhaps more good can be done by the December 1st Movement if they encoded their language before it totally disappeared and was wiped out by Afrikaans, English or Xhosa.

Actually Iron Age communities have been present in Southern Africa at least as far back as 200 AD. Other even more aboriginal Africans in the area are the Khoisan ethnicities. North of the 5S latitude these hunter-gatherer groups have often been described as pygmies, in the South they are designated as the Khoi Khoi and San. Intermarriage and cultural interpenetration between the Khoisan and Bantu language speakers has been going on from the earliest times. This is particularly noticeable in the languages of the Khoisan themselves and the Xhosa-Zulu, Tswana-Sotho, Nama and the Berg Damara (7). It needs also to be added that major migrations have taken place in the region and beyond over the past centuries. As early as AD 1000 the two main strands of the Bantu languages in South Africa were discernible, the Nguni and the Sotho. Iron, copper and gold were produced. Complex social systems with state structures were in existence in the southern African region as the Luba and the Mutapa or its predecessor the Great Zimbabwe state. This latter maintained trade relations on long distance basis as far as the Mozambican coast. In the northern reaches of the region during the 15th century Shona influence and power was considerable under the Mwana Mutapa kings (8). The Portuguese who were the first Europeans in the area came into contact with these societies. The Portuguese circumnavigation of the Cape at the end of the 15th century opened the way to western contact to the southern most tip of the continent. The Portuguese however made no settlements. As Davenport has pointed out although the French, English and Dutch East India Companies considered the possibility of establishing posts at the Cape, in the end only the Dutch did (9). After the initial period of regular trade and barter between the Dutch sailors and the Khoikhoi dating back to the early 1600s, by the 1650s relations had soured. Serious conflict broke out in 1659. In 1672, in response to land hunger of the colonists, the company "purchased" a large tract, including all the lands, forests, pastures, rivers and creeks, from the Cape Peninsula to Saldanha Bay from two Khoikhoi chiefs. The payment we are informed, was made in brandy, tobacco, beads and merchandise valued at 10 pounds (10). From 1673 to 1677 the settlers started a military campaign against them. The effects of war, decimation, deprivation of land and livestock increasingly forced the Khoikhoi into the position of labourers for the Dutch colonists (11). J.H. Hofmeyer, Smuts' Deputy Prime Minister writes:

> Finally the white man's disease completed the
> process. In 1687 there was a fever epidemic, in
> 1713 and again in 1755 small-pox ran riot.
> Leprosy followed, and arrack and brandy carried
> on the work (12).

About 400 West African slaves were introduced in 1658. Soon after this in 1667 the Dutch East India Company started bringing in slaves from the Indian coast, Java, Ceylon, East Africa and Madagascar (13). The offspring of the Dutch and the Khoisan, and the various groups of slaves were the beginning of the contemporary Cape

Coloured community. J.A. Hesse has published findings to strengthen the argument that hundreds of the leading Afrikaner families have in the past intermarried with non-whites (14). This latter fact is reality which racially sensitive Afrikaners, the "pigmentalists" or "pigmentocrats" have great difficulty confronting. In his *Inside Africa*, John Gunther observed that; "miscegenation has taken place in the past, and this no doubt is what makes the Afrikaners so fantastically sensitive about colour. South Africa is a country where people do not like to have their family trees too carefully scrutinized" (15).

The Tensions of Identity

The so-called Coloured of South Africa form about 10 percent of the population of the country. 80 percent of this category live in the Cape where time and numbers have helped create a vibrant and westernized, largely urban sub-culture which is original to this part of Africa. The popularization, idiomatic creativity, subtlety, and development of Afrikaans has grown with the Coloured population. Indeed, the Afrikaans language as the original patois that it was, emerged out of the Cape Coloured community. In an article which appeared in the *Cape Times* of 30th October 1996 (*Boere Don't Own Afrikaans*), Prof. Ampie Coetzee an Afrikaans Literature Professor of the University of the Western Cape pointed out that, "It's a funny thing.... This language, Afrikaans, has been portrayed as the language of the oppressor, the language of the Boere.   But it wasn't the language of the Boere - ever - it was simply a language the Boere used.   In fact, it was always the language of black and coloured people - and now this movie (*Skerpioen Onder Die Klip*) actually proves it. It's very well researched". Phillip Van Niekerk's article, *Wie se taal? Wie se kultuur?* which appeared in the *Weekly Mail & Guardian (Johannesburg)* sometime ago, draws attention to Achmat Davids research findings that, "Afrikaans, the language of the white tribe of apartheid, is a black tongue".

Evidence suggests that the proportion of Afrikaans speakers among the Coloured has relatively expanded since the ascendancy of Afrikaner nationalism. The first Afrikaans newspaper, *Die Afrikaanse Patriot*, appeared in 1876, under the sponsorship of the *Genootskap van Regtes Afrikaners* (the Society of True Afrikaners) (16). The first Afrikaans book to be published appeared in 1861, two more were published by 1873, there were 3000 in 1937 and 10,000 by 1954 (17). Writing in 1965, R.E. Van Der Ross pointed out that in the ten year period between 1955 and 1965, the change in favour of Afrikaans was remarkable.

> Whereas 20 years ago the Afrikaans medium secondary school was a rarity, and the Afrikaans medium high school was non-existent, the picture today is totally different. To a degree, this has been the result of the expansion of secondary and high schools in the country areas....But there also seems to be little doubt that in the Cape Peninsula, stronghold of the Coloured people, the process of Afrikanerizing the schools has been artificially accelerated (18).

This was of course in line with the ultimate objectives of the apartheid regime. The Broederbond which has always remained its heart and mind since its foundation in 1918, according to one of its earliest members L.L. du Plessis, was created to advance the status of the Afrikaans language (19). Whilst the language was spread and cultivated by the Afrikaner nationalists as a matter of policy, it was also their view that the language "belonged to them". For them, the strategic objective, that is, the social dominance of Afrikaans was essentially seen as being in the exclusive service of the Christian, Nationalist, Calvinist, White, Afrikaner. The explosion of the viability of the myth of language dominance came to a definitive end in June 1976. Eslanda Goode Robeson, the Afro-American anthropologist and celebrity (wife of Paul Robeson) quickly observed among her co-passengers travelling to South Africa in 1936 that; "*Native* is their word for our *nigger*; *Non-European* for our *Negro*; *European* means white; and *South African* , surprisingly enough does not mean the millions of original black people there, but the white residents born there, as distinguished from white residents born in Europe who are called *colonials* or *settlers*" (20).

As Wilkins and Strydom have indicated, when Vorster as Prime Minister closed the chapter on Coloured representation in parliament in 1968, "the Broederbond was ecstatic for indeed the ultimate dream of the secret society had been achieved". In their shortsighted understanding of the historical process, the segregation of all coloured races domiciled in South Africa with provision for their independent development under the trusteeship of whites had been in their mistaken view assured (21). Jan Esterhuyse has rightly noted that on the whole the Coloured community has in the past been generally aloof from the "language-nationalism" (taalnasionalisme) and the "peoples-nationalism" (volksnasionalisme) of the Afrikaners. Writing in 1986, he points to the fact that, "..die groepe vandag nog 'n kille onbetrokkenheid handhaaf" (22). This disinterestedness which Esterhuyse refers to in this Afrikaans quote is attested to by others. Jakes Gerwel can be called into evidence for his contention that the way the language question in South Africa has historically developed has been used as a political instrument for the white Afrikaner constituency, and that indeed, the whole question of language struggle and language sentiment is a whiteman's question. His words are that; "die hele kwessie van taalstryd en taalgevoelens 'n 'witmens'-kwessie is" (23).

According to 1991 figures, the total population of the South Africans classified under the old system as Coloured numbered 3,286,000, of which 2,795,000 are to be found in the Cape Province, 311,000 in the Transvaal, 104,000 in Natal and 71,000 in the Free State. Out of the overall figure, 2,081,000 are based in the Western Cape (24). Sub-sets of the wider Coloured group are often acknowledged. These include the Cape Malay, the Griquas, and the migrants who moved in the 19th century into South West Africa (Namibia) described as Rehoboth Basters.

In du Plessis' study of the Cape Malay, he pointed out that: "... In Cape Town the terms 'Malay' and 'Mohammedan' are often used as synonymous; but strictly speaking 'Malay' stands for that section of the local Muslim community in which the descendants of Malay slaves and political exiles are to be found". 80 percent of the Muslim are Afrikaans speaking. The other 20 percent of the Muslims are made up of Muslims of Indian extraction. For both sections of the Muslim community in the Cape, "Arabic is the language of the Mosque", Urdu for the Indians and English that of greatest convenience. Most of the Cape Malay are of the Sunni Sect (25). Du Pisani describes the Rehobothers (Basters) as the predominantly Afrikaans-speaking descendants of Khoi mothers and Afrikaner fathers in the Northwestern Cape (Namakwaland) who crossed the Orange river in the second half of the 19th century and settled in the Rehoboth area in South West Africa (Namibia) in 1870 (26). One of the outstanding testimonials of how oppression and the terms of its rationalization, handed down by the oppressor to the oppressed, can be internalized and accepted without question, is the way in which in Namibia the so-called Basters (Bastards) use that self-designation without appreciating the insult attached universally to the term.

Davenport indicates that, some groups of Khoikhoi and Coloured retreated into the interior in the face of settler penetration. They included preeminently groups led by Adam Kok from Piketberg and his descendants and Barend Berends. They were encouraged by the London Missionary Society (LMS) to settle in their stations and at Griquatown. Furthermore, they were later persuaded to adopt the designation "Griqua" instead of "bastard", "in recognition of the Grigriqua (Khoikhoi) element in their make-up" (27).

Further afield in the Southern African region in Zimbabwe, Botswana and Swaziland the term Eurafrican has also been used to define those "coloureds" whose African antecedents are more easily acknowledged. In Swaziland, Botswana and Zimbabwe many of them speak African languages. In South Africa proper, generally African ancestry is often denied, although in a recent radio interview during the period of the elections (April 1994) Neville Alexander suggested that about 80 percent of Coloured people have some African roots. It is likely that, in coming years, the increasing numbers of the coloured group who speak African languages and acknowledge their African roots will increase. On the 15th of September 1994, the Pan Africanist Congress General-Secretary Benny Alexander set the cat amongst the pigeons by thrusting the issue to the fore of public debate. Changing his name from Benny Alexander to Khoisan X, he made the point that changing his name was a statement against racism and colonialism. "The former colonialists, upon their arrival, behaved like gods and recreated and renamed everything after themselves....it is therefore necessary that racist colonial names, symbols, statues, river names, city names, airport names...be removed" (28). He would remain with this new name, until his historical root has been traced. This is unfolding, at a time when South Africa as a whole is discussing what to do with the abundant monuments of Apartheid. In response to a lively debate which emerged, Adam Small observed:

> Benny Alexander (Khoisan X) rebels against this "tradition", in the lineage of which his "!Khoi African" roots were regarded as being "heathen and barbaric". And his attitude is obviously an attitude of: to hell with them; I will be what I am....More correctly: I will at last try to be what I should have been in the first place (29).

The denial of African historical connections is a phenomenon which is understandable in the context of a society which had for centuries been constructed on the basis of pigmentational stratification running roughly parallel with class divisions. The reinforcement of class by colour and occupational differentiation invested strong caste-like characteristics to the general features of social life. With the Coloured category ranging from "black" to "white", socio-economic pressures and the benefits of white privilege made the "graduation" into white status for those who could on account of the lightness of their skins do this often succumb to the temptation. Van der Ross writes that;

> It is not true that all Coloured people who are fair try for white. And where it is true, it is often also true that they cannot be blamed. For they do not try for White for the mere sake of whiteness, but for the sake of better job opportunities, the better education, the better social outlets, which are offered to those accepted as White (30).

Another observer, Howard Brotz remarked that because of the marginalization and alienation which the apartheid system created, "this marginality only inflamed the desire of those who could do so to pass for White, which was eating the soul out of the Coloured people" (31). Reliable statistics for the phenomenon is difficult to come by. However, the existential problems attendant on this result of institutionalised racism in South Africa have been sociologically aggravating. Elsewhere Van der Ross writes that amongst those who secretly "upgrade" themselves across the colour divide;

> Very often this process of safeguarding one's position entails severing connections with previous associates to whom one is known as coloured. This means that one has to break off old friendships, leave the district where one has grown up, and in many cases it has even meant leaving the country. I do not want to go into the question of personal and inward suffering which this state must entail. The breaking of old associations is at no time easy, and then there is the constant threat of discovery. Every Coloured person, in the towns particularly, could tell of numerous cases of people who have "turned white"-- and who have not gained the sympathy of their erstwhile friends in doing so. The many cases on record of divisions within families, often tragic, always with unhappy results, represent but a small part of the many actual cases (32).

At the other end of the spectrum of the Coloured population, Africans particularly among the Xhosa-speaking groups upgraded themselves in the apartheid ranking system by "passing" as Coloured. In such instances, the adoption of an Afrikaans name (e.g. changing Ntimkhulu to Grootboom) and the speaking of Afrikaans became the way in. Again here the attractions of relative privilege and social mobility were the key motivating factors.

The top end of the apartheid social scale had its own share of the contradictions of the system. After the establishment of the Immorality Legislations which forbade sexual contact between the various colours of South Africans, "Illicit sex", and its various consequences became a regular source of embarrassment for whites, particularly colour-conscious Afrikaners. Such liaisons sometimes led to suicides by those whose licence, and weakness of flesh in this respect one way or the other came to light (33).

With regards to the whole issue of "race classification" under apartheid, the *Verligte* (enlightened - less conservative) National Party politician Dawid de Villiers admitted the truth of the South African Institute of Race Relations finding that, "much humiliation, anxiety and resentment has resulted from official investigation into such cases". In some cases of reclassification from white to coloured or from coloured to black African, "those concerned may have to change their homes, their jobs, their children's schools" (34).

In a society dominated by white racism, the Coloureds who are westernized tended to internalize dominant "white" values. The colour scheme of white dominance has had a profound effect on the attitudes of Coloureds to colour. S.P. Cilliers in his study, *The Coloureds of South Africa* (1963) remarks that;

> It was noticeable, however, that Coloureds attached more value to hair form than to skin colour, since the Bushman and Hottentot also have relatively light skins. A light skin did not necessarily indicate white ancestry, while a dark skin could be due to slave ancestry. Since the slaves were of "higher" cultural development than the aborigines, slave ancestry was not despised. Hair form, however, was a more accurate indication of "primitive" or "civilised" origin. Pepper-corn or frizzy hair could only signify aboriginal ancestry, which came to be despised. Straight hair signified white or slave "blood".

A 1974 study, *Sosio-Politiek Houdings Van Stedelike Kleurlinge* in 1974, found out that 72.2 percent of the respondents reacted positively to the notion of a "Coloured identity". This feeling of "Coloured" identity was weaker in Cape Town than in other areas. The majority of educated people rather significantly, did not identify positively with the notion of a "Coloured" identity. However those above the age of 50 tended more to do so. The majority rejected the "non-white" identity, "Coloured" was more acceptable, but most preferred to be simply regarded as South Africans (35).

In South Africa the concept of ethnicity has been directly employed in the rationalization of the apartheid scheme. The limits of its scientific usage has been stretched to give respectability to the racist system. Neville Alexander writes that;

> the way in which the ideologues of the National Party use the term "ethnic group" makes it almost impossible for any serious-minded

person grappling with these problems to use the term as a tool of analysis (36).

In the South African context this point can hardly be disputed. But the South African situation is an extremely unique case in the whole world. Elsewhere, in another discussion, Alexander advances the argument that;

> ethnic groups do not exist: and since "ethnicity" is an attribute reputedly possessed by "ethnic groups", it follows *a fortiori* that it is, in the happy phrase of Terence Ranger, an "invention". There is no logical reason whatsoever to argue for the existence of entities called "races" or "ethnic groups" simply from the fact of racial prejudice or ethnic awareness of whatever kind (37).

Certainly, the notion of race is a bankrupt idea. There are no groups which from Adam have existed in some "untouched" condition of purity. Race as a concept has no scientific usage today, in South Africa or anywhere else. It is used in South Africa largely as part of the conceptual arsenal employed by the Apartheid system. When it is used it is meant to refer to physical attributes, mainly the colour of skins and hair texture. It is a term which is regarded with the utmost distaste by enlightened people. The concept of ethnicity is a different kettle of fish, it is the central area of anthropology. Kinship systems, belief systems and religious practices, languages, cultural value systems, and other customary usages exist. They are not fictitious.

Ethnicity actually diverges sharply from the race concept. Ethnicity in a serious sense has no reference to physical appearance. Strictly speaking it refers to cultural attributes of groups which have commonality in language, customary practices, religion, sometimes geographical locality and history with mythology which often imposes a subjective reference point for those who share the specific cultural attributes in question. In no instance are the contributing qualities which give character to a specific ethnicity duplicated in exactly the same respect for other ethnicities. It has tended to be used in reference to actual or supposed precapitalist groups, but in correctness it should refer to all historico-cultural units independent of the mode of production in which they are structured.

Ranger's argument in his paper, *Missionaries, Migrants and the Manyika* (1983), is spot on with regard to the way in which anthropologists, missionaries and colonial elements have created or "invented" "tribes" in Zimbabwe. The Akan were likewise split into Akim, Fanti, Ashanti, Nzima, and Akweapim in Ghana; in the Sudan, the Bari-speaking people were chopped-up into Bari, Nyangbara, Fajelu, Mondari, Kakwa, and Kuku. The Dinka became, Atwot, Gogrial, Bor, etc. From the Senegal river are to the Cameroons along the Sahel, the Fula or Fulbe are given about nine different names. As Alexander indicates Ranger finds the invention of Shona "tribes";

> through the activities of an amalgam of social agents comprising missionaries and their converts, African labour migrants and later, colonial officials, chiefs and others...By cutting up the Shona language continuum into different dialect zones and freezing each dialect through transliteration and through the production of Bible translations, hymn books, catechism, printed collections of folklore, stories, etc, languages--and in the course of time corresponding ethnic identities-- such as Chimanyika, Chizezuru and Chikaranga were literally invented (38).

The above case is unquestionable, and as I have indicated there are numerous other similar cases in Africa to support the general thrust of the argument. Leroy Vail makes the equally apt point that; "empirical evidence shows clearly that ethnic consciousness is very much a new phenomenon, an ideological construct, usually of the 20th century, and not an anachronistic cultural artifact from the past" (39). But one must be careful not to throw out the baby with the bathwater. Neocosmos has produced an argument which I share.

> The historiography of "ethnicity" follows most contemporary social science in general and social anthropology in particular in conceiving of "ethnicity" as a specific consciousness. In fact the terms "ethnicity" and "ethnic consciousness" are used interchangeably in these writings. While in most cases it is recognized that an "ethnic" consciousness cannot be understood in terms of itself, the general approach seems ultimately to be caught up in a notion of ethnicity

as "imaginary", or perhaps to be influenced by a form of vulgar marxism for which only class differences are somehow "material" while other differences are simply "ideological". The problem of course, is that it thus becomes very difficult to establish the social basis of this consciousness and hence to explain its existence (40)

Doubtlessly, the material conditions of our social existence directly informs our consciousness but this consciousness is dressed up in a cultural and historical setting. Class conflict and contradictions do not work themselves out in a culturally and historically disembodied fashion, lacking historical and cultural specificity. What is important for the analyst to dissect is the convergence or divergence of class and ethnicity in each instance of ethnic manifestation in class societies. Not all expressions of ethnic interests are automatically "unprogressive" or reactionary. In societies where ethnicity/nationality more or less parallels class differences, the class struggle is often manifested as an ethnic or national struggle. But ethnic sentiments can also become instruments for the manipulation and control of constituencies by groups whose interests are narrow and anti-socially protective. Because of their trans-class character ethnic qualifications are easily mobilized sentiments which blunt class consciousness.

Asiwaju has drawn attention to other ways in which the "invention" of tribes and ethnicities were contributed to by the colonial experience. His particular reference point was the effects of the colonial partition in the creation of different names for the same people across borders.

> Thus for the people who were called Yoruba in British Nigeria, the name in French Dahomey (now Benin) is "Nago", which sometimes assumes the characteristic masculine and feminine forms of Nagots and Nagottes. Other examples, again in relation to Nigeria are the Gude, the Higis and the Matakam who on the Cameroonian side of the border in the area of the ancient state of Mandara came to be called respectively the Djimi, the Kasiki and the Wula. Other examples include the Kpelle and the Loma in Liberia, referred to respectively as the Guerze and Toma in French Guinea, the Baydyranke in French Guinea or Guinea-Conakry, called the Bambaraca in Portuguese Guinea or Guinea-Bissao (41).

Coloured in Post-Apartheid Society

The term Coloured is not an ethnic or cultural designation. It attempts to define people on the basis of physical appearance, particularly skin pigmentation. Under the apartheid system it was a mischievously convenient way of protecting the racist type of white privilege constructed around a capitalist industrial system. The architects of apartheid supported and indeed encouraged the Afrikanerization of the whole society particularly the Coloured while at the same time denying the appropriation of the culture which those with white skins shared with those with darker pigmentation, described as non-whites. In his attempt to define the Coloured identity, Van der Ross plays into the hands of the Apartheid ideologues by producing a definition purely based on colour.

> Because we are the result of so much mixing, it is difficult, indeed impossible, to define our limits. There is a large central core of people whom it is easy to identify from physical characteristics, but there are no clear, definite boundaries, as we merge into and with all other groups in varying degrees. That is why, of all South Africans today, we have the least sense of identity. But a person's identity is largely what that person considers it to be (42).

The contradiction between consciousness and false consciousness is not a point much disputed even by social scientists who are not marxian inclined. Needless to say, identity has both objective and subjective dimensions. But what is more problematic in the above quotation is that the author makes no reference to culture. A German may look no different from a Dutchman or Swede but their identities as they perceive these in an ethnic sense would be quite different. These differences are purely cultural and historical. Elsewhere, Van der Ross suggests that; "the very fact that people refer to the Coloured people, means that there is a certain identity as a population group". The term population group is a typical apartheid notion which is conveniently blurred, but in the South African context is well understood as referring in the first place to colour. The fact that "Coloured" is an invention of the racist ideology of the South African system cannot mean that it should be accepted as a universally accredited term. From the late 19th century till the mid-1950s, in North America and the United Kingdom, the term "Coloured" was used by Americans and the British to describe anybody who is "non-white". From the mid-1950s onwards it was regarded by people thus described as an insulting categorization. Today, no where in the world is the idea of "Colouredness" used as the primary point of identification of people. Van der Ross goes on to suggest that;

> ...when people refer to themselves as "we, the Coloured people", or as "ons Bruinmense", they are using an identifying term, just as some people refer to themselves as "we Xhosa's", or within the larger Xhosa group, as "we AmaHlubi's"...(43).

The major mistake here is that Xhosa is not an identity based on "race", it is hardly recognizable in a person's face or hair texture. It is purely a cultural reference point of identification. The problem appears to be tied up with the fact that although in all important cultural respects, the so-called Coloured shares the same terrain as the Afrikaner, hitherto the Apartheid system has by fascist contrived theory and practice restricted the normal or universal application of culture as a reference point for identification to exclusive white monopoly usage and hence deliberately suppressed the emergence of a wider consciousness of the Afrikaner identity amongst the so-called Coloured. The frustration and alienation caused by the racist rejection of people whose culture is in many respects, at least for the majority Afrikaans has been a long-standing and festering wound on relations between cultural siblings. The results of the investigative commission of the South African Bureau for Racial Affairs (SABRA) published in May 1964 by the University of Stellenbosch, and compiled by Prof. Erika Theron revealed this crisis of alienation in the various reports of most of the contributors. Why has the white Afrikaner establishment so steadfastly resisted the recognition of the wider Afrikaner identity? One possible explanation for this is the fact that, the appropriation of the Afrikaner identity by the so-called Coloured would shift the heart of Afrikanerdom from the privileged white basis it currently enjoys to a wider basis which would demystify the myth of a white Afrikaner volk. In this sense the expansion of the designation of Afrikanerdom to cover all cultural Afrikaners is part of the democratic and anti-racist process of post-apartheid society.

The process of deracializing Afrikanerdom, is first and foremost currently an intellectual debate which is engaging the minds of all concerned parties as new symbols of democracy and cultural space become issues of great debate and intellectual ferment in South Africa. In order to deracialize Afrikanerdom, Afrikaans would need to be hegemonized by the masses in the Cape Flats, in Namakwaland and other similar concentration areas of the masses of Afrikaans speakers. In its pace-setting, it would need to move out of the drawing rooms of the racists who have for so long dominated its usage.

This ferment is not without its contradictions and dilemma. Adam Small in inimitable style comments that;

> ...I have never wished to --and could never-- deny the existential category of "being coloured".....Never, of course, have I maintained that coloured are "a homogeneous cultural community". That, certainly, is a nonsensical idea (44).

Some of the academics like James Ellis of the University of the Western Cape, have resistance to the notion of sharing an identity with a social group which they regard as having been responsible for so much inhumanity, repression and social conflict. In discussions Ellis has suggested that "forty years of apartheid socialization" is responsible for this.

About 75 percent of the Coloured people speak Afrikaans as mother-tongue. Most of the rest speak English. Most of those who speak English can also speak Afrikaans. There is a smaller number who speak African languages. There is evidence among students of the wish to assert African historical credentials with the citation particularly of Khoi Khoi, Nama and to a lesser extent Xhosa antecedents. In a fact-sheet put out by the *African Youth Movement* in 1994, they make the point:

> We therefore reject with contempt derogatory labels like Goffels, Mestico or Coloureds as we believe such terms are meant to instill self-doubt and self-hatred in our people and further harm their

psychic and physical being. In response to the image imposed by the oppressor we use the term Khoisan as our frame of reference, as we see ourselves as self-defined and not defined by others.

The global villagisation of the human community is increasingly going to mean that the various peoples and cultures of this world will interact more. The mixing of people which has been going on from time immemorial will increase. As Sir Learie Constantine put the case almost 50 years ago: "Mixed marriages have been going on ever since humanity first occupied the earth, so it is unlikely that they will stop now that communications are more developed than ever before" (45). This is however unlikely to increase the number of ethnicities of the human community. There is indeed rather, a danger of the opposite, the extinction of increasing numbers of languages and cultures. The fate of Khoi Khoi and San languages are under pressure. The recent *Atlas of World Languages* (1993), suggests that, almost a third of the worlds existing languages is spoken by less than a thousand people in each instance.

In other parts of Africa e.g. Ghana among the Akan there are people who in appearance would be in South Africa described as coloured. They are described as Akan, but depending on the issue under consideration, they could be referred to as *o'bri* literally meaning "lightskinned". It is a categorization which has a significance not too different from being tall, short, fat or small. In the hierarchy of identities which prevail in social intercourse the cultural categorization of being Akan or in the sub-units created by colonial anthropology (and the social elements Alexander and Ranger refer to), Twi, Fanti, Akweapim, Akim or otherwise, *O'bri* is a secondary attribute with no ethnic or cultural reference. In East Africa, the coloured in the sense that the term is used in South Africa are probably for the majority Swahili-speaking and are in the first instance so described.

In a sense, in as far as the problem of identity is concerned, the black Afrikaner or so-called Coloured has been the worst victim of the system of Apartheid. At the opening ceremony in 1996 of the *December 1st Movement* (named in remembrance of December 1st 1834, the date on which slaves were freed in the Cape, and conceived as a movement for the search of roots among the Coloured), the Rev Michael Weeder made the point that, Coloureds had become "the step-children of history". White minority rule and the racist rejection of cultural siblings has left a mark on this section of the South African citizenry which would need time to correct. Popular perceptions suggest that, the effects of centuries of a racist culture cannot be effaced overnight. It is often argued that racist attitudes will die with the current adult population. One point that can be made without fear of equivocation is that, the democratic process will however in the long run erode the legacy of racism. Euphemistically, the day South Africa reaches the point where being an Afrikaner becomes a notion free from racial connotations, and becomes an identity about which people can be proud and unashamed, South Africa would indeed have successfully put behind it, the legacy of "race". By the same token, the so-called Coloured will have to come to terms with their African history, origins and belongings, in order to make the Afrikaner (black and white) African.

In an article which appeared in *The Weekly Mail & Guardian (Johannesburg)* of 3rd September 1993, under the title; "Why be 'So-called'? Be Real and Proud", Anthony Whyte of the Department of History, University of Cape Town, reacting to an article by Paul Stober of August 20th in the same paper wrote that: "That Paul Stober should invite fellow 'so-calleds' to unite organisationally under a 'big C' Coloured banner (*Mail & Guardian, Johannesburg,* Aug 20-26 1993) reveals the deep ambivalence exhibited by so many in the coloured community regarding their own African heritage. 'So-calleds' such as Stober should recognise and celebrate the fact that a good deal of their own genetic material derives from the Khoikhoi and San peoples, Africans who occupied the Cape thousands of years before Europeans or Nguni speakers entered the region...... Stober and his fellow 'so-calleds' should consider reimaging themselves as Africans, as Khoi. They need fear no recriminations in thus privileging the African component of their diverse ethnic heritage; selective 'amnesia' of this kind is the stuff of identity formation at the level of race, people, nation or volk" (46). The intellectual ferment which will lead to redefinition of identity is on. In September 1996 *The Cape*

Cultural Heritage Development, an organisation which aims to reconstruct coloured people's indigenous culture, art and tribal ethnicity, was registered in Cape Town. David Andrews, spokeman for the group which is made up of community members from across the Western and Northern Cape provinces, said the idea was to restore people's Cape cultural heritage to its former pre-1652 glory. Andrews remarked: "The Griqua nation and other Qua tribes have consistently clung to our Khoisan identity, even in the dark years of apartheid when we were classified against our will as coloureds" (47).

In the future, doubtlessly there increasingly will be more and more "Coloured" who speak African languages as mother-tongue, and have other African cultural attributes, new or old, which they whole-heartedly identify with. This development will ultimately expose the lie of 'Colouredism". All this will eventually take the Afrikaner, black and white, beyond "the colour line".

Notes

1. The introduction of this paper draws on an earlier paper; see, K.K. Prah. "South Africans: The People, and the Problem. A Historical Survey". In, EDESCA Publication; *South Africa: Current Events Seen Against the Historical Background.* Harare. 1988.

2. Indian South Africans form about 3 percent of the population of the country. They were brought into the country as indentured labourers for the sugar plantations in Natal from 1860 onwards. Poor treatment and gross exploitation of the Indians was instituted right at the beginning of their presence, and indeed in 1872, the Natal Legislature rather half-heartedly attempted to redress some of these ills. Indian immigration increased slowly from about 10,000 in 1875 to 100,000 by the end of the century. White racism has regarded Indian labour as a threat and restricted employment and occupational opportunities for this community. The threat of repatriation has always been bandied around. Since 1914, about 50,000 Indians have been repatriated under various arrangements. For decades, there were restrictions to travel and residence in the Transvaal, the Orange Free State and the Cape. See Frene Ginwala. *Indian South Africans*. Minority Rights Group Report. No.34. London. 1977. T.R.H. Davenport. *South Africa, A Modern History*. Jo'burg. 1987 edition. p.117. See also, C.J. Ferguson-Davie. *The Early History of Indians in Natal*. Johannesburg. 1977. P.S. Joshi. *The Tyranny of Colour. The Indian Problem in South*

Africa. Durban. 1942. A recent edited text which summarizes the current position of Indians in South African society is provided by; A.J. Arkin, K.P. Magyar and G.J. Pillay. *The Indian South Africans*. Pinetown. 1989.

3. After the Anglo-Boer war, the Milner administration in response to increasing and festering African dissatisfaction and rejection of mine labour, decided to import Chinese indentured labour. About 60,000 were imported. This labour group proved invaluable to the mining industry, but at the same time the myth and fear of the racist notion of "yellow peril" was raised in both the United Kingdom and South Africa. As a result, in 1906 after the ascendancy of the Liberal government in the UK, the import of Chinese labour was terminated and within 5 years almost all the Chinese were repatriated.

4. See Muriel Horrell. *Legislation and Race Relations*. SAIRR Publication. Johannesburg. 1971. pp.9-13.

5. L. Louw and F. Kendall. *South Africa: The Solution*. Bisho. 1986. p.31. In a publication, *Die Naturellebeleid van die Nasionale Party onder Hertzog, Malan, Strijdom en Verwoerd* (No date) by G.D. Scholtz, evidence is thrown up to show that the policy of apartheid was theoretically laid out long before 1948 by a string of white Afrikaner leaders like Hertzog, Malan, Strijdom and finally Verwoerd.

6. C.P. Mulder. "Address to the World Affairs Council". Los Angeles. 6th June 1975. *The UNESCO Courier*. November. 1977. p.10. Quoted here from Marianne Cornevin. *Apartheid, Power and Historical Falsification*. UNESCO. Paris. 1980.

7. Indeed, the extent of these cultural-linguistic admixture among the Bantu and the Khoisan is much too profound and interpenetrated to be simply a few centuries old. In a private conversation, the Bishop of Kimberley and Kuruman, Bishop Winston Ndungane informed me that, the traditional name of the Khoi Khoi is Ngwai Ngwai, that Khoi Khoi is a corruption of that. G.M. Theal writes that; "The Hottentots termed themselves Khoikhoi, "men of men", as they prided themselves upon their superiority over the other race with which they were best acquainted...the Bushmen...". See, *The Beginning of South African History*. London. 1902. p.19.

8. See, S.I.G. Mudenge. *A Political History of Munhumutapa c1400-1902*. Harare. 1988.

9. T.R.H. Davenport. Op cit. p.22.

10. M. H. de Kock. *Economic History of South Africa*. Cape Town. 1924. p.13.

11. T.R.H. Davenport. Op cit. p.25.

12. Jan H. Hofmeyer. *South Africa*. London. 1932. p.42.

13. M. H. de Kock. Op cit. p.15. See also I.D. du Plessis. *The Cape Malay*. Cape Town. 1944. p.3.

14. See, M. Attwell. *South Africa. Background to the Crisis*. London. 1986. p.22.

15. John Gunther. *Inside Africa*. London. 1955. p.456. Gunther adds that; "I heard a Coloured leader say (no doubt he was exaggerating), 'If people with any trace at all of black blood were excluded from parliament, half the members would have to walk out". There are even Afrikaners who joke about the subject, and say to their friends lightly, 'Ah, you suspect black blood in me'". Ibid.

16. See, Conor Cruise O'Brien. *Passion and Cunning*. New York. 1988. p.143.

17. Ibid. p.455.

18. R.E. Van der Ross. "Afrikanerizing the Coloured". *Cape Times*, 26th January 1965. In, *Coloured Viewpoint*. Compiled by J.L.Hattingh and H.C. Bredekamp. Bellville. 1984. p.265.
Van der Ross' suspicion of the National Party government's intentions in this respect went further. He argued for example that; "another way in which this process is being hastened is the manner in which Coloured authors who write in Afrikaans are lionized. Some of them are not unaware of the possible motives behind this, and many a wry remark is made in these august circles about their recognition....as Kleurling digters..".Ibid. p.266.

19. See Ivor Wilkins and Hans Strydom. *The Broederbond*. London. 1979. p.45. Elsewhere, the authors draw attention to the fact that; on January 1934 a circular letter in the names of Prof. J.C. van Rooy and Mr. I.M. Lombard, chairman and general secretary was distributed which pointed out to all bond members that, their key object should be the "*Verafrikaansing* of South Africa in all aspects of life....Let us focus our attention on the fact that the primary consideration is whether Afrikanerdom will reach its ultimate destiny of domination (basskap) in South Africa". Without doubt, this idea has been an important ingredient in the ideology of white Afrikaner baaskap. In the lexicon of the Apartheid ideologues, *Verafrikaansing* is indeed another word for the hegemonization of South African society by the white Afrikaner. Ibid. p.60.

20. Eslanda Goode Robeson. *African Journey*. London. 1946. p.29. Her designation of the meaning of "South African" for only whites was correct. Where she goes wrong is that, the term non-European referred to Asians, Coloured and Africans. There is evidence of overlapping usage of these "racial" categories in the South

African context. Sometimes there is usage of the terms "coloured" and "other coloured" these latter being non-Cape Coloured. In a book published in 1946, it is stated that; "In the Orange Free State the words 'Coloured People' are often used for the natives, and vice versa". The Natal Law XV, of 1869 defined a coloured person as "a Hottentot, a Coolie, a Bushman, a Lascar, or any other people commonly called Kafirs". See, Eric John Dingwall. *Racial Pride and Prejudice*. London. 1946. p.129.

21. Ibid. p.162.

22. Jan Esterhuyse. *Taalapartheid and Skoolafrikaans*. Emmarentia. 1986. p.8.

23. Jakes Gerwel. *Literatuur en Apartheid*. Bellville. 1983. Quoted here from J. Esterhuyse. Ibid.

24. R.E. Van der Ross. *100 Questions about Coloured South Africans*. Cape Town. 1993. p.6.

25. I.D. du Plessis. Op cit. p.1. In a recent study by Y. da Costa the researcher found out that, "On the basis of an empirical study of attitudes of Muslims towards other religious groups, it appears as if Muslims in the Cape Peninsula prefer to associate primarily with their own group, and with religionists rather than with non-religionists, with Christians rather than with Jews or Hindus, and with Hindus rather than with Jews. This suggests a possible tendency in religious groups to prefer their own groups for association, and to place other religions at different social distances away from themselves". See, Y. da Costa. "Religious divide in the Cape Peninsula: A Study of Socio-religious Distance between the Muslim Community and other Religious Communities". In, *South African Journal of Sociology*. Volume 25. Number 2. May 1994. p.55.

26. A. Du Pisani. *South West Africa/Namibia: The Politics of Continuity and Change*. Johannesburg. 1985. p.10.

27. T.R.H. Davenport. Op cit. p.25.

28. See Benny Alexander becomes Mr. X. *The Argus*. 15th September. 1994.

29. Adam Small. New !Xhoisan X ID not a naive move. *Sunday Argus. Sunday Focus. Weekend Argus*. September 17/18 1994.

30. R.E. Van der Ross. *Coloured Viewpoint*. Op cit. p.153.

31. Howard Brotz. *The Politics of South Africa*. Oxford. 1977. p.121. "Passing" has of course not been restricted in historical experience to the so-called Coloured of

South Africa. In equally recent times, it has been not infrequent in the United States amongst African-Americans. The process both in the USA and South Africa were practically the same i.e. moving house or out of town (or indeed emigrating), breaking or cutting off all links with your darker consanguines, changing your name.

32. See, R.E. Van der Ross. "The Coloured People". In, Prudence Smith (ed). *Africa in Transition.* London. 1958. p.172.

33. It is arguable that the recent (1993) highly publicised link between former senior Afrikaner politician and Broederbond secretary Piet Koornhoff and the Coloured lady Ms. Marcelle Adams would have been hardly imaginable 20 years ago.

34. See, Dawid de Villiers. *The Case for South Africa.* London. 1970. p.91. The differentiation has been made since the early 1970s between Verligtes and Verkramptes among Afrikaner nationalists. The former are literally "the enlightened" or so-called moderates or liberals amongst them, and the latter refer to the more hard-line pro-apartheid conservatives.

35. See, *Sosio-Politieke Houdings Van Stedelike Kleurlinge in 1974. Onderneem namens die Kommissie van Ondersoek na Aangeleenthede Rakende die Kleurlingbevolkingsgroep.* UNISA. Pretoria. November. 1974. p.7.

36. N. Alexander. *Sow the Wind.* Braamfontein. 1985. p.46.

37. Ibid. p.147.

38. Ibid.

39. Leroy Vail quoted here from M. Neocosmos. "Agrarian and 'Ethnic' History in Southern Africa: Beyond a Nationalist Analysis". Mimeo. 1991.

40. M. Neocosmos. Ibid.

41. A.I. Asiwaju. *Partitioned Africans. Ethnic Relations Across Africa's International Boundaries. 1884-1984.* London. 1985. p.3.

42. R.E. Van der Ross. *100 Questions...* Op cit. p.5.

43. Ibid. pp.13-14.

44. Adam Small. "Let's Get Together to Talk of Racism and Education". *Sunday Focus. Weekend Argus.* June 18/19. 1994.

45. Learie Constantine. *Colour Bar*. London. 1954. p.96.

46. See, Anthony Whyte. "Why be 'So-called'? Be Real and Proud" *The Weekly Mail & Guardian (Johannesburg)*. September 3rd to 9th, 1993.

47. See, Joseph Aranes. "Reviving the Proud Culture of the Khoi: Group in Search of 'Nation's Soul'". *The Cape Argus*. 20th September 1996.

The Subvention of the Invention of Africa

Colonialism is dead!
Long live the new colonialism
Flagged with the banner of universalism
under western tutelage...(Kwame Walata)

I want to be free and equal
But cannot leave old master...(Anon)

Introduction

It is unfortunately not often that scholarship on Africa, or rather by
Africans on Africa, both in Africa and in the diaspora, which
scintillates, gemlike, or soars in stature, in compositional intricacy and
verbal facility appears for public consumption. We are referring in
this respect not only to language and expressiveness. Rather, we are
thinking more of the organic character of the knowledge which is
presented and its encyclopedic breadth, the sheer volume of its
learning, and its ability virtually to stand, blow by blow, the best that
can be called into comparative witness from anybody, anywhere else
in the world. The regular feature of African scholarship has been
possibly more often rather spare on learning and encyclopedia, and
too often, over-generous in textual and facile philosophical
regurgitation. Mudimbe's text, *The Invention of Africa* is exceptional
in learning, reading and presentation.

Mudimbe sets himself in this text, a task and a half, and rises to the
occasion as a master of his concerns and much of what he surveys, in
spite of the fact that there are important and significant weaknesses in
his overall position and in some matters of detail. As he says in his
introduction;

> ... the book attempts,... a sort of archaeology of African
> *gnosis* as a system of knowledge in which major

philosophical questions recently have arisen: first concerning the status of traditional systems of thought and their possible relation to the normative genre of knowledge. From the first chapters, which interrogate Western images of Africa, through the chapters analysing the power of anthropologists, missionaries, and ideologists, to the last, on philosophy, I am directly concerned with the processes of transformation of types of knowledge (Intro. page X)

Mudimbe is as much an artist as he is a thinker, and I mean it here in a complimentary sense, although, there are those who may argue to good effect that the two categories are essentially mutually exclusive. Whichever way one looks at it, one clear and undeniable steadfast fact about the inventor of "The Invention of Africa" is that almost giraffe-like, he stands with his doubtlessly exceptionally erudite text, a head and a long neck above the academic lilliputians and the scholastic pedestrians who happen to be too many for any good in contemporary Africa. Like a giraffe, he sees very far and very well but sometimes misses the reality of his immediate universe. Like an archaeologist he unearths buried and forgotten knowledge and experience embossed and enshrined in priceless cognitive artifacts.

At the discrete analytical level, where isolated notions and elements of discourse are scrutinized, Mudimbe comes out with full marks and flying colours. He disentangles propositions and contextual imperatives with skills and a mind subtly imbued with dialectical finesse and verbal propriety. It is at the level of synthesis that he falls short. The analytically disentangled pieces are not sufficiently glued back, the epistemological jig-saw puzzle never achieves the sort of unity which permits the reader to concretely conceive Mudimbe's philosophical bearing conclusively.

The Chemistry of an Eclectic

Mudimbe's prodigious reading in a sense overwhelms him. One loses his views in the views of others. Sometimes, the readiness to refer to sources is taken to a fault. For example, (page 92) in the middle of the text, Mudimbe points out that, "the political image of Africa after 1965 is indeed distressing. Authoritarian regimes have multiplied, rules and norms of democracy have been flouted or rejected". We are referred to Gutkind, Wallerstein, O'Meara and Carter. What is said is so well known and so well understood by any observer of contemporary African history that, one is at a loss to see why credit is given to the above authors with regards to these views. On the same page, we are told "Toure was isolated in his dictatorship and Nkrumah, challenged and insulted, died in exile". We are referred to Erica Powell. Erica Powell, in her autobiography reveals a lot about her long service to Nkrumah which is to say the least very revealing, interesting and informative. But, the above points brought forward by Mudimbe are common knowledge. Do we need Erica Powell to know this? Mudimbe could have as well simply stated this.

He appears overeager and too ready to call others to witness by a selective evidential method, in which key confirmatory or disputative passages are recalled with albeit a precision which the best surgeon operating on the human body would be hard put to rival. His witnesses, whether for the prosecution or the defence say just what and how much he wants them to say, not one word more or less. This is of course superb craftsmanship. But, the whole message or evidence of such witnesses is lost. In effect, too many of them say what they do not really intend on the whole to say. Such procedures are artistically permissible. They form the substance and technique of the collage. But, as a scientific mode it is dodgy or, to say the least, contentious. For some it may appear to be a technique of over-summarization of more detailed and complex issues. For others it may be almost heretical. But heresy may be historically a viable course of progress.

The implicit philosophical basis of such notional collation which Mudimbe is obviously a master of and has crafted to such eloquent sublimity, is eclecticism. While it permits the richness and ideological tapestry of a philosophical Tower of Babel, it excludes conceptual and methodological consistency. As Marvin Harris noted years ago in his *The Rise of Anthropological Theory*, "eclecticism is certainly the path of least resistance through the frequently strident polemics of the system-mongerers".

What however needs to be pointed out is the fact that, not all eclectics consciously adopt such positions in order to avoid the minefield of argumentation with nomothetic thinkers, system-builders and "grand-theoreticians". Many are philosophical sceptics who are generally suspicious of whatever may appear to be all-embracing approaches to scientific analysis. Others are plain inductionists who prefer "multi-dimensional" approaches inspired by the use of "all available techniques". In the introduction to his study, Mudimbe invokes the views of Foucault to attest to his approach. He writes that;

> ....from a methodological viewpoint I think, as Foucault put it, that "discourse in general and scientific discourse in particular, is so complex a reality that we not only can but should approach it at different levels and with different methods". For this essay, I have chosen an archaeological perspective that allows me to address the issue of the progressive constitution of an African order of knowledge. However, for reasons having to do with the bizarre nature of some of the sources used, mainly the anthropological ones, I have preferred not to distinguish the epistemological level of knowledge from the archaeological level of knowledge. (Introduction. pp.Xl-Xll).

The spontaneist and volitional approach to methodological issues is grounded ultimately in philosophical quicksand. Eclecticism collates and catalogues, without a firm systemic grid. Thus for Mudimbe, the Belgian scholar B.Verhaegan "is both a Marxist and a Catholic" (page 178). There is here apparently no contradiction. Fanon, Mudimbe suggests was "a solid Marxist" (page 92). Fanon like many of his generation was affected by the existentialist thinkers, and also Hegelianism and Marxism, but he can hardly be described as "a solid marxist". The limits of his theory of nationalism and culture, the Sorelian character of his concept of revolutionary violence reveal wider philosophical affiliation than "solid marxism".

Few social scientists in recent years, have pointed to the pitfalls of eclecticism with the succinct and unmitigated forthrightness of Harris. He writes:

143

Eclecticism,....abounds with hidden dangers. In practice, it is often little more than a euphemism for confusion, the muddled acceptance of contradictory theories, the bankruptcy of creative thought, and the cloak of mediocrity. It bestows upon its practitioners a false sense of security and an unearned reputation for scientific acumen. Science consists of more than responsibility to the data; the data must be responsible to theory. Neither one without the other suffices. It is impossible to be faithful to the facts and at the same time indifferent to theory.(2)

Technically, Mudimbe is an analytical mind of exquisite quality. But because of his philosophical eclecticism and the theoretical limitations or impositions of this, the continuity of analyzed units of discourse is undermined and ruptured. The collation as a thought-continuum is segmentary and ultimately truncated. This weakness runs almost consistently throughout the text, except to a much lesser degree, in his discussion on, "The Missionary Discourse and Africa's Conversion" (The Power of Speech), where the philosophical and analytical integument of his exposition is systematically liberated and achieves consistency and homogeneity.

Mudimbe's reading of the debates triggered by Tempels's *Bantu Philosophy*, Griaule's work on the Dogon, and the reactions of Mbiti, de Hemptinne, Kagame, Diop, Tshiamalenga, Dieterlen and de Heusch is succinct. His conclusion here can hardly be faulted:

I am personally convinced that the most imaginative works that reveal to us what are now called African systems of thought, such as those of Dieterlen, de Heusch, and Turner, can be fundamentally understood through their journey into *Einfuhlung*. In the case of African scholars, it often becomes a case, as with Kagame correcting Tempels, or sympathy towards oneself and one's culture (page 145).

The "journey into *Einfuhlung*" we must remember started from "the primitivist tradition". In itself it represented progress within its own historical context i.e. the late colonial period. It is a journey almost as distant as the journey from evolutionism to functionalism. Kagame,

144

Lufuluabo, Mujynya and Mulago are not mere intellectual gobemouches of Tempels. In sympathy with their cultures which have for so long been denigrated by the westerner, they attempt to polish in the context of their historical conjuncture the then new approach to "the other". They claim a gnosis which will authenticate and rehabilitate their culture especially in as far as ontological issues are concerned. They ultimately together with most of the ethnophilosophers, the negritude philosophers and *negrologues*, belong to the populist ideological mould which in the era of late anti-colonial and early post-colonial nationalism articulated the strength of populist consensus and Afrocentric reaction to retreating western colonialism. Idealization of the past is a hallmark of populism. Indeed the "retrojection" which Towa accuses the ethnophilosophers of is a classic feature of the populist ideological edifice (page 158). They share together with the functionalists one major weakness among others. This is that, they are methodologically ahistorical, creating reified and timeless images of the African reality reconstructed within the framework of "the ethnographic present".

The methodological and substantial crudities of Tempels and his disciples's contributions to the analysis of African traditional thought systems, do not detract from, in the first place, the need to undertake this task, and secondly the considerable degree of preoccupational centrality which these issues continue to enjoy in the African mind in the post-colonial era. Obviously, *weltanschauungen* in themselves do no constitute composite philosophical constructs, but they are subject to philosophical analysis. I would go as far as suggesting that they represent primary areas of concern if the enterprise of philosophy in Africa is to engage the essence of African culture, society and history. In other words there is little point in Africa philosophers simply integrating themselves into western concerns and competing for audience on the western preoccupational platform. The analytical tools may well be universal, but the point of focus must have historical and sociological relevance. We are saying that, Socratic philosophy was not concerned in sociological focus about issues in China; the Utilitarians were concerned with issues of emergent western industrial society; the Existentialists were responding to the *angst* inherent in modern western society; the Enlightenment philosophers were in the main preoccupied with considerations which found expression in the French Revolution and its aftermath. We are here in agreement with Mudimbe when he places the issues raised by Eboussi-Boulaga on the origin, identity and being of the African, on the critical philosophical agenda (page 153).

Hountondji's demolition of the ethnophilosophical position has been sound, and Mudimbe accords him careful attention. But, the weakness in Hountondji's position, his willingness to identify his position both formally and contextually essentially within the western epistemological field has rightly opened him up to criticism for western dependency and neo-colonialism. When Hountondji announces with aplomb "we have produced a radically new definition of African philosophy, the criterion being the geographical origin of the authors rather than an alleged specificity of content" (page 159), he in one fell swoop attempts to obliterate the contradiction between the universal and the specific; the specific being "the invented Africa". The message is that, there is nothing worth the name in the African field, join the so-called universal philosophical crusade under western eyes. Elitism would be a misnomer for Hountondji's disease, unless his accusers see both themselves and the accused as part of the western intellectual world. Mudimbe's discussion of the thinking of African clerics shows close familiarity and sound understanding and his mind appears to be at its best in these sections of the text (The Patience of Philosophy).

One area in this text where the absence of clear philosophical bearing and an absence of methodological coordinates is most emphatically felt is in his analysis of some of the principal "socialist" leaders Africa has seen since the era of independence, and his discussion of "Marx Africanized". In Senghor's system "anthropologists' speculations are inter alia, combined with Marxism"; in Nkrumah, the "African Personality ideology gave rise to the ambiguous social philosophy". We are told that, "when prominent leaders such as Senghor or Nyerere propose to synthesize liberalism and socialism, idealism and materialism, they know that they are transplanting western intellectual manicheism" (pages 184-1850). I am not so sure if they know this. The ambiguity of these philosophical concoctions can be understood essentially within the concept of populism. The mixing of political ideological strands in the name of African Socialism is a feature of the class character of the dominant groups which have over the past three decades supervised the post-colonial state in Africa.

To Be or Not to Be

At heart, Mudimbe's study wrestles with a number of key propositions struggling to achieve the status of plausible assumptions. Very early in his text, our attention is drawn to the fact that, "until now, Western interpreters as well as African analysts have been using categories and conceptual systems which depend on a Western epistemological order". Undeniably, he explains, as any serious examination of the facts will reveal, "even in the most explicit Afrocentric descriptions, models of analysis explicitly or implicitly, knowingly or unknowingly, refer to the same order". This order, in foundation and historical edifice has created "the other", a beast which is neither fish nor fowl. The invention of this unicorn as Mudimbe amply shows was part of the western encountering experience, and nearer our times colonialism in particular. The inventors were not only the adventurers and travellers of earlier times but also the more intellectually astute and trained minds who dabbled in colonial anthropology.

From Herodotus, Diodorus of Sicily, and Pliny of classical Europe through John Lok in the 16th century, the western mind has been satisfied to feed on the idea of Africans as not quite human. Some were "people without heads, having their eyes and mouths in their breast". Others were, "headless, satyrs, strapfoots" still others, were "cave-dwellers who have no language and live on the flesh of snakes" (page 71). As Mudimbe points out, the 19th century anthropologists were evidentially firm in their depiction of "the essential paradigm of the European invention of Africa: Us/Them". No lesser a figure as Herbert Spencer upheld the view that:

> According to Lichtenstein, the Bushmen do not "appear to have any feeling of even the most striking changes in the temperature of the atmosphere". Gardiner says the Zulus

"are perfect Salamanders, arranging the burning faggots with their feet and dipping their hands into the boiling contents of the cooking-vessels"(3).

Attention can also be drawn to another not insignificant figure in anthropology, Lewis Henry Morgan. Carl Resek has pointed out that in 1850, concerning the fate of Africans in America, he expressed the view that;

> ....it is time to fix some limits to the reproduction of this black race among us. It is limited in the north by the traits of the whites. The black population has no independent vitality among us. In the south while the blacks are property, there can be no assignable limit to their reproduction. It is too thin a race intellectually to be fit to propagate and I am perfectly satisfied from reflection that the feeling towards this race is one of hostility throughout the north. We have no respect for them whatever (4).

Levy-Bruhl's prelogical primitives, Malinowski's acculturating and detribalized natives, are all part of the order of "the other". During the heyday of the African independence movement in the early part of 1959, the cultured English writer Evelyn Waugh was peddling as recollections of his travels and adventures in Africa and, as part of what he had learnt about the eastern coast of Africa during a visit; that in the 16th and 17th centuries, when Arabs, Turks and Portuguese were contending for over-lordship of the East African coast particularly around Mombasa and Malindi;

> ....for several years a ferocious cannibal tribe from south of the Zembesi, called the Zimba, had been making a leisurely progress up the coast, eating their way through the inhabitants. They appeared on the mainland just as the Portuguese fleet anchored off the island. The Turks invited the Zimba to cross over and help against the Portuguese. The Zimba came, ate the Turks and, gorged, shambled away to the north, leaving Mombasa to the Portuguese. They were repulsed at Malindi and disappeared from history (5)

148

When the evolutionists and diffusionists in the nineteenth century, and later the functionalists in the twentieth century brought the African from the back of beyond, it was to "repress otherness in the name of sameness", strip "otherness" of its more conceptually outlandish and atavistic baggage and in effect attempt to "fundamentally escape the task of making sense of other worlds" (page 72). While arguably, both Anglo-Saxon functionalism and Gallic structuralism are inherently teleological and represent a move from emphasis on "the other" towards "the same", the point which Mudimbe does not make is the fact that this escape is not accomplished, not because of sheer "limiting ethnocentrism" or "epistemological determinism". The creation of "the other" was a western project, the unification or synthesis of "the other" and "the same" historically and dialectically represents the negation of "the same" as a western product. The new sameness cannot historically be inspired by the old sameness but by its historical anti-thesis. I would emphatically add that this process historically has an intermediate stage or position, where "the other" has an epistemological order for-it-self. It is only when and after "the other" defines itself for-it-self that the epistemologically useful negation of occidento-centric scholarship comes historically on the agenda. I shall revisit this point.

Mudimbe, goes to considerable extent in his search for the route forward to an epistemological universalism which will historically outdate upstream the limitations of the past. He cautiously suggests:

> It is surely possible, as functionalism and structuralism proved, to have works that seem to respect indigenous traditions. And one could hope for even more profound changes in anthropology,....

Mudimbe is obviously not very convinced himself that indeed functionalism and structuralism respect native traditions. They "seem to respect" are his words, and indeed they only "seem to respect" the native and his/her lore. The native is no longer six months or a year away from London, in Equatorial forests or harsh deserts, as distant from western civilization as the earth is from the moon. The native is only a few hours flight from London. The conditions of his/her life

149

and mode of livelihood, directly affects the life of the westerner in the depths of the concrete jungles of the western world.

Stories about man-eating Zimbas sweeping along the East African coast and eating all humans on sight cannot be pressed into currency however ostensibly authoritative the source may be in the age of the radio and television. Functionalism pleads that the native can and should be understood in his/her own cultural or societal context. The native is different but not a monster, he/she is a neighbour and we know that he/she does not have eyes in the breast. He/she remains "the other" although less conceptually remote. As Harris observatively notes, between 1930 and 1955, the overwhelming majority of studies and contributions of the structural-functionalist school was grounded in fieldwork undertaken in European controlled Africa, particularly in the British administered territories. He points out that,

> Under such circumstances it is impossible not to draw a connection between the proposal to study social systems *as if* they were solidary and *as if* they were timeless, with sponsorship, employment, and indirect association of the members of this school by and with a now defunct colonial system (6).

In both Fortes and Evans-Pritchard's *African Political Systems* (1940), and the Introduction to Forde and Radcliffe-Brown's *African Systems of Kinship and Marriage*, we are advised that these texts are not merely for anthropologists but also those involved in colonial administration. The point must not be lost on us that, "the other" in the era of functionalism is the colonized or neo-colonized. Structuralism as we know it today, is very considerably a contribution of the French anthropological tradition. Like functionalism, its roots lie with Durkheim, with the continuity rendered in the work of Mauss particularly in *The Gift*, and subsequently by his student Levi-Strauss who refined the methodological underpinnings of the approach to excellence in *The Elementary Structures of Kinship*. Levi-Strauss the giant of French structuralism recognizes the binary character of structure for the anthropologist and his/her study object or phenomenon. The native remains "the other" an object of western creative genius, scrutiny and rationalization. As Homi Bhabha has eloquently put it, "an authorized version of otherness" (7). Mudimbe is of course right when he points out that;

> .... so far it seems impossible to imagine any anthropology without a western epistemological link. For on the one hand, it cannot be completely cut off from the field of its epistemological genesis and from its roots; and, on the other hand, as a science, it depends upon a precise frame without which there is no science at all, nor any anthropology (page 19).

I would go as far as saying that, the western epistemological genesis and link will remain. It cannot be denied or wished away. Mankind can only be thankful for it, whatever its shortcomings may be. It is part, but only part of the raw material for a future universal epistemological fund and subject to radical reinterpretation. What is more important is what African scholars, or for that matter non-western scholars do with it. In as far as western epistemology autonomously defines "the other" from its own Eurocentric crucible, "the other" remains a caricature, a Caliban of the western mind. As Bhabha would have it, "a reformed recognizable Other, as *a subject of a difference that is almost the same, but not quite*" (8). It is only through the scholastic counter-penetration of the existent epistemological field that the dialectical process towards universalism is completed. No amount of facile, faithful or clever mimicry would resolve this contradiction. But how is this to be achieved?

Mudimbe addresses this problem only in bits and pieces, fighting shy of the fuller and more profound implications of the problem. Summoning the voice of Levi-Strauss and the spirit of Rousseau, he proclaims that, "nothing is settled; everything can still be altered. What was done, but turned out wrong, can be done again. The Golden Age which blind superstition had placed behind (or ahead of) us, is in us" (page 34). He then attempts to resolve the contradiction between "the same" and "the other", by invoking Paul Ricoeur's *cri de coeur*, inviting us under the inspiration of the sign of Plato's "great class" which itself "associates the Same and the Other. The Similar is the great category. Or better, the Analogue which is a resemblance between relations rather than between simple terms" (9).

I would argue that Ricoeur's outspoken epistemological conscience given the intellectual currents and trends of our times in the western world represents a voice in the wilderness. Carl Sagan's epistemological ethnocentrism with regards to Sagan's denial of the historico-cultural authenticity of Dogon cosmology in respect to their Sirius mythology is more in character with western images of the African even today. There is still much life in "the belief that scientifically there is nothing to be learned from, them, unless it is already ours or comes from us" (page 15) (10).

For Mudimbe, Foucault's wish to interrogate the western will to truth and restore to discourse its impact as an event, and "abolish the sovereignty of the signifier"; and Levi-Strauss's attempt to conceive empirical categories that can be used as keys or indicators "to a silent code, leading to universals", break the initial ground for the crusade towards the unity of "the same" and "the other". Mudimbe's discussions here and in this respect, read more like articles of faith, than the result of dialectical processes, and smack of what I describe as "epistemological millenarianism"; the conception of a methodologically sensible future in which the epistemological field is an actively common heritage of mankind, but without a plausible or credible route to it.

The discussion on Blyden is rich and resourceful. But because Mudimbe does not examine Blyden's ideas from a historically analytical perspective, the evolution of Blyden's thought is lost. On a whole range of issues, including Islam, Christianity, African nationalism, native culture and colonialism, Blyden's views were never static. They changed. A fuller appreciation of Blyden cannot be achieved unless it is structured firmly in a historical matrix.

The presentation of Ethiopian Sources of Knowledge, as an appendix, tags on rather ungainly to the tail-end of the study. This is unfortunate, given its analytically exciting possibilities. A mind like Mudimbe's would have possibly satisfyingly dissected it to be gorged by African scholarship.

The text has its occasional factual slips. I shall provide two examples. On page 76, we are told about "....the first monographs of African laws and customs", and then referred to Ajisafe and Danquah. Certainly, Sarbah and Casely Hayford pre-date these efforts (11). Another such slip is on page 45, where we are wrongly informed that, "the mass celebrated on the Guinea Coast in 1481, under a big tree displaying the royal arms of Portugal, symbolized the possession of a new territory". The Portuguese actually, were in;

> La Mina on the 19th January 1482. On the following morning they suspended the banner of Portugal from the bough of a lofty tree, at the foot of which they erected an altar, and the whole company assisted at the first mass that was celebrated in Guinea..(12).

Concluding Remarks

Mudimbe has produced a masterpiece in scholarship on Africa. The solidity of his learning, his acutely analytical mind, the richness of his discourse, and his courage to address central and daunting issues facing African scholarship are laudable.

There are of course as indicated, weaknesses in the exposition. To my mind the most sensitive, indeed the Achilles heel of his work lies with the choice of the concepts of "the same" and "the other". In his search to find what many will agree is a desirable objective i.e. the basis of a universal epistemological reference point in the study of society and Africa in particular, Mudimbe's ultimate position is vague. As we have earlier stated, the dialectics of this process requires that initially, "the other" consciously constitutes itself for-it-self as an autonomously self-defining source of episteme. It is this step which will create the basis of the negation of the Occidento-centric focus of what today is the epistemological field. It is only when the negation has been effected that the basis of a common universal epistemological heritage can be put in place. As Mpoyi-Bwatu, N'Zembele and Willame have urged Mudimbe, he needs "to draw the political implications from his conclusions" (page XI). The cultural dimensions of the "national question" are lost on him. As I have frequently insisted, the use of African languages constitutes a missing link in any move forward in African intellectual and scholastic progress.

Mudimbe (also Hountondji) wants ultimately to become international without being first national, in a historical situation where "the self" of the African has never since the penetration of the west been allowed to exist, or even coexist, except as a mimic man. "The other" is a mimic man.

Notes

1. Marvin Harris. *The Rise of Anthropological Theory*. New York. 1968. p.284.

2. M. Harris. Ibid. p.285.

3. Herbert Spencer. *Principles of Sociology*. (1876). 1906 Edition. New York. Vol 1. p.50. Further on in the same text, while discussing what he considered to be the limited intellectual capacities of primitive peoples he recalls Sir Richard Burton into evidence; "....with Negroes. Burton says of the East Africans, 'ten minutes sufficed to weary out the most intellectual' " (Ibid. p.83).

4. Carl Resek. *Lewis Henry Morgan: American Scholar*. Chicago. 1960. p.63.

5. Evelyn Waugh. *A Tourist in Africa*. London. 1960. p.49. He writes elsewhere that concerning the Islands of Kilwa Kisiwani, Songo Mnara and Sanji ya Kati, "The Persians probably came here first and set up a dynasty in the tenth century. It was under the Arabs of Oman that the place became great. The Portuguese came there at the beginning of the 16th century. In *1589* (my emphasis) the Zimba ate all the inhabitants and left a waste that was irregularly reoccupied. (Ibid. p.75). Waugh attributes the authenticity of the story to   Mr. Kirkman (the well-known Archaeologist); who "exuberant enthusiast for the comic as well as for the scientific aspects of his work" (p.48),....."gleefully recounted" (p.49)...."This vivid little history was conveyed to us....with infectious but inimitable zest by the Director of Antiquities ". (p.51). James S. Kirkman is hardly unique. Hamo Sasoon in a review of Kirkman's, Fort Jesus: A Portuguese Fortress on the East African Coast. Clarendon Press. 1974. informs us that, "Dr.James Kirkman spent twenty-four years on the coast of Kenya, and of these, fourteen were spent in Mombasa focusing (to quote Sir Mortimer Wheeler) his "skill and almost infinite labour" upon the history of the great Fort". See *Azania. Journal of the British Institute in Eastern Africa*. Vol XI. 1976. p.196.

6. M. Harris. Op cit. p.516.

7. Homi Bhabha. "Of Mimicry and Man: The Ambivalence of Colonial Discourse". *October*. Cambridge, Mass. No.28. Spring 1984. pp.125-133.

8. Homi Bhabha. Ibid.

9. P. Ricoeur. *The Reality of the Historical Past*. Milwaukee. 1984. p.25. Quoted here from Mudimbe. Op cit. p.34. Ricoeur's awakening is well recalled by Mudimbe; "The fact that universal civilization has for a long time originated from the European centre has maintained the illusion that European culture was, in fact and by right, a universal culture. Its superiority over other civilizations seemed to provide the experimental justification of this postulate. Moreover, the encounter with other cultural traditions was itself the fruit of that advance and more generally the fruit of Occidental science itself. Did not Europe invent history, geography, ethnography, and sociology in their explicit scientific forms .....When we discover that there are several cultures instead of just one and consequently at the time when we acknowledge the end of a sort of cultural monopoly, be it illusory or real, we are threatened with destruction by our own discovery. Suddenly it becomes possible that there are just *others*, that we ourselves are an 'other' among others". P. Ricoeur. *History and Truth*. Evanston. 1965. pp.277-278. Quoted here from Mudimbe. Op cit. pp.19-21.

10. I recall with cynical hindsight my experience in Cape Coast University, Ghana, 1974-75, where in the Department of Anthropology and Sociology, a young American Africanist with a smattering of Twi (Akan) was supposed to be teaching the Social Structure of the Ashanti/Akan to undergraduates. This phenomenon is as absurd as visualizing an African sociologist teaching German students in a German university in Bavaria, the social structure of Bavarian society. Scholarship today would regard in all likelihood the former example as "normal" or acceptable. Indeed, this is precisely the route to an eventual chair in "African Studies" in the western world. The latter case is likely to provoke laughter at the patently surrealistic.

11. See, John Mensah Sarbah. *Fanti Customary Laws*. London. Ist Edition. 1897. Joseph Ephraim Casely Hayford. *Gold Coast Native Institutions*. London. 1903.

12. See N.O. Anim's contribution on Ghana in, D.G. Scanlon (ed). *Church, State, and Education in Africa*. New York. 1966. p.168. Also, R.M. Wiltgen. *Gold Coast Mission History: 1471-1880*. Techny. Illinois. 1956. p.16.

Accusing the Victims - In My Father's House

Review of Kwame Anthony Appiah. In My Father's House. Methuen. London. 1992.

Introduction

Those of us who as young adults or youngsters saw before our eyes, the ripening of the independence movement and its first fruits in Africa, and have lived to see the fruits turn bitter, are often inclined to look for scapegoats, whipping-boys and culprits to interrogate and flog, for the mess that has befallen the independence dream. A glowing dream which has turned into a tragi-comic nightmare. Many point to the generation immediately preceding us, who it is argued, enjoyed and wickedly corrupted the society that we inherited from the colonialists. Others go further down the line, to deposit blame at the doorstep of earlier antecedents. A few hyper-disillusioned voices, prophets of doom and damnation, cry that we are accursed, and even fewer suggest that we are pitched in the darkness before dawn, the darkest hour. Almost all agree that we must critically appraise the past, in order to see and work more confidently towards a better tomorrow. It is in this latter spirit and with this emphasis, that Appiah's alluring text is written.

When we question the past, and subject its assumptions to dispassionate scrutiny, we do this not with the purpose of reliving the sentiment of Oscar Wilde; pursuing an art for its own sake. We do it in all seriousness and recognize the importance of being earnest, in order to produce workable answers for the trials and tribulations of developing Africa.

Appiah's text unites a number of essays clustered around four central issues. The two opening chapters attempt to identify racial thought in the founding ingredients of Pan-Africanism, particularly in the work of Alexander Crummell and W.E.B. Du Bois. The two subsequent chapters trace out issues of African identity in the work of literary figures, particularly Wole Soyinka. The next two chapters discuss modernity and the language of postmodernism. The last cluster of chapters focuses on the dynamics of identity and its politics. There is a lot of meat on the bones of Appiah's discourse. But he unselfishly provides a lot of scope for those who have bones to pick with him. Appiah's reading is encyclopedic and he successfully unites the thematic components of the discourse that he assembles in this text.

Appiah writes from a rare and unique position. He writes of himself:

> If my sisters and I were "children of two worlds" no one bothered to tell us this; we lived in one world, in two "extended" families divided by several thousand miles and an allegedly insuperable cultural distance that never, so far as I can recall, puzzled or perplexed us much. As I grew older, and went to an English boarding-school, I learned that not everybody had family in Africa and in Europe; not everyone had a Lebanese uncle, American and French and Kenyan and Thai cousins. And by now, now that my sisters have married a Norwegian and a Nigerian and a Ghanaian, now that I live in America, I am used to seeing the world as a network of points of affinity (p.ix)

Much less than one percent of contemporary humanity can make this sort of claim to the universe. In the coming century and beyond, an increasingly greater deal of humanity will become like this. In a way, it is the distant future of humankind. The world will become a village of consanguines. But we are still rather far from that order of things. And we should be careful not to make for the present, however desirable we may consider the case to be, the world seen from that vantage point, everybody's world. It simply isn't so. We live in an economically and politically lopsided world, in which some of Appiah's consanguines are happier than others; a world in which by and large, some of the "points of affinity" live off the sweat and labours of others, and have made a history of this. Equally importantly, we should be careful that vantage point does not unduly influence the way we see the world in general and Africa in particular. In other words, we should be able to take a proper distance from ourselves in our consideration of others, and not make our reality everybody's reality. Otherwise we may willy nilly, end up accusing

157

the victims in father's house. Those who fight bullies are not bullies. Appiah is sufficiently circumspect, intellectually prudent and candid to admit that:

> It would be foolhardy to suppose and unpersuasive to claim that in such a situation it is always one's dispassionate reason that triumphs, that one can pursue the issues with the impartiality of the disinterested. Precisely because I am aware of these other forces, I expect that sometimes along the way my history has not only formed my judgement ... but distorted it... (p.xii)

Although this passage appears in the preface, it is in fact an afterthought. It has been penned *post ipso facto*. It is a realization after the fact, and there are many who will possibly regard it as an excuse, if not a lame one.

The *Pas de Deux* of a Shy Postmodernist

In his father's house Appiah gives exceptional and full rein to his mother's tongue. Technically, the most remarkable feature of Appiah's writing is that he oscillates between two stylistic approaches. On one hand, a lean, mean and clean prose, shorn of unduly contrived frills and obvious semantic embellishments; a textuality which is clinical and logically sanitised and which achieves a superb refinement, thereby investing his product with a unique aesthetic status of unrivalled dimensions, in spite of the sinewy verbal facility he presses into service. Most of the text is presented in this steely fashion. On the other hand, specifically in Chapter 7, where he runs headlong into the murky depths of postcoloniality and postmodernism, he swings into the opposite mould, and indulges in a not unextravagant display of postmodernist language of construction and deconstruction which will put to shame the most fashionable exponent of this genre. In either instance his message is elusive, and deliberately so. He is one moment here and the next moment there. A philosopher without a clear philosophy, he fleetingly iconizes only to pillorize in the next breath. He provocatively flirts with postmodernism only to flee in fear and terror from its philosophical licentiousness. The fundamental flaw in Appiah's work is that there is no philosophical position or ground on which he is prepared or able to pitch his tent. Philosophically he belongs everywhere and nowhere. There is greater wisdom in Muhammad Ali's strategy of floating like and butterfly and stinging like a bee, but also being able to rope-a-dope. If you deliver you must also be able to take.

Appiah, in obvious suspicion, distances his acute analytical sense and logic from the implicit intellectual hegemonic culture of contemporary Euro-American post-modernism on African and other Third World realities. He writes:

> Sara Suleri has written recently, in *Meatless Days*, of being treated as an "Otherness-machine" and of being heartily sick of it. If there is no way out for the postcolonial intellectual in Mudimbe's novels, it is, I suspect, because as intellectuals - a category instituted in black Africa by colonialism - we are always at risk of becoming Otherness-machines. It risks becoming our principal role. Our only distinction in the world of texts to which we are latecomers is that we can mediate it to our fellows. This is especially true when postcolonial meets postmodern; for what the postmodern reader seems to demand of its Africa is all-too-close to what modernism - as documented in William Rubin's "Primitivism" exhibit of 1985 - demanded of it. (pp.253-254).

Here, Appiah's Africanist instinct and nerve is holding its own. If we press that logic further, we can say that, sure enough, as creatures of Prospero's magic, the intellectual Calibans of western culture, we serve more than we are served. As Claude McKay will have it, we "bend our knees to alien gods who hold us in fee". We are created more to imitate than innovate. Our autonomy is defined for us, and we are confined within the specifications and conditions of our birth and cultural baptism. But a couple of lines down the road, he intellectually caves in. Considering the role which postmodernism might play in the Third World, his verdict is "... it is, I think too early to tell". Why is it too early to tell? His answer is this; ... "what happens will happen not because we pronounce upon the matter in theory, but out of the changing everyday practices of African cultural life". This is a loose reflection. True enough, truth emerges more out of social practice than cerebral gyrations, but history is the substance of practice, and all social sciences are ultimately sciences of history. We have seen a chain of western philosophical vogues come and go, and their transformatory impact on African cultural practices have been at best restricted to a narrow elite of African philosophical initiates, who have regurgitated these canons in a variety of forms too faithful to their western sources to be of much relevance to the realities of African culture and society.

For those of us like Appiah, who have the benefit of middle age and hindsight, we recognise that we have in our formation been subjected to successive intellectual fashions born in the west. These intellectual fads have affected successive generations of African intellectuals and shaped their thinking on Africa and the world, but have hardly provided viable inspirational or ideological sources for transformations which translate into the betterment of the quality of life of African humanity.

African intellectual borrowing from the west has been more formal than organically integrative with respect to the African historical and cultural baggage. Over the same period, Asia has been doubtlessly more successful and triumphant. Asia is not faithfully reproducing western intellectual rages and crazes at each new historical twist and turn. Asian cultures have, like all living cultures, been importing and exporting culture, but what change is taking place is historically selective and grounded in their own usages. I need to remind the reader that nowhere in the societies of the substantial "Asian Tigers" is the phenomenal development we are seeing constructed in the language of former colonial or imperial masters.

During the late fifties when youthful voracity brought us to the world of ideas, existentialism - and its trendy beat culture with Jack Kerouac and Norman Mailer, "hipsters" to boot, with Dizzy Gillespie (the man with the periscope trumpet) and Charlie (the Yardbird) Parker bebopping and rebopping all the way - imposed its own logic on our minds. From either Nietzsche, Heidegger, Kierkegaard, Camus or Sartre many of us took our cue.

By the beginning of the sixties, Sartre had through a philosophical marriage of convenience opened the door very invitingly to the ghost of Marx as a stalking and haunting shadow. We let him in, but not without Levi-Strauss and his structuralist language getting also a foot in. Analytical philosophy extending from logical positivism was largely an Anglo-Saxon affair, which for many who enjoyed the confidence of continental Europe was a nit-picking dry philosophical school, addicted to the pedantic analysis of solecisms, and devoid of the panache and florid richness of Gallic sententiousness and German solidity. In the language of the pontiff of the English language F.R. Leavis; "a Wittgensteinian enterprise ... produces gratuitous logic, gymnastic fatuity, unprofitable conclusions and intellectual frustration" (1). The burial of structuralism and the birth of post-structuralism did not hound Marxism. out of the turf, rather, it constituted a counterpoint to neo-marxian essentialism which kept the contemporary generation earthbound.

A number of tendencies were discernible in the marxism of the late sixties and early seventies. There was firstly, the hack marxism of the Soviet state and its ideologues. In contrast to this was the militant Chinese advised position which, outside the Soviet orbit, attracted much of the pro-revolutionary Third World. There was thirdly also a critical western marxism which directed its venom mainly at the Soviets. Fourthly, there was a loud "new left" position which tended to lean on Trotskyist views associated with the Fourth International. Marxism in Africa, except possibly in the case of Amilcar Cabral's PAIGC (Party for African Independence in Guinee Bissao and Cabo Verde) has never fully become a theory and practice adapted to the concrete realities of African society. On the wider theoretical field, much of the late sixties and early seventies saw a three cornered contestation between neo-marxism, structuralism and post-structuralism. Many of us were still "underground" not because we loved Hades but because "God was still dead". In that era of "flower power", there were many who, like the tormented Dostoievskian hero Ivan Karamazov, readily challenged society with: "Once God is dead, does not everything become permissible". The permissive society was in full swing. We saw it, "happenings" and all from *Mokkum* (the affectionate Yiddish term for Amsterdam, or "Jerusalem of the North").

161

By the early and mid-seventies the new high-priests of ideas in the west were chanting the funeral dirges of post-structuralism and neo-marxism. (On the African continent however, marxism continued to attract the academic class until the collapse of Soviet-sponsored institutionalized marxism). During the late seventies and early eighties postmodernism evolved from an *avant garde* position into a fully fledged tradition, thanks to the tenacity of Foucault, Derrida, Deleuze and Baudrillard. Its initial ascendancy as largely a French project was in a sense an affirmation of the much acclaimed centrality of French culture as the heart of western civilization. Indeed, most of the post-2nd World War intellectual fashions have been preeminently French.

Postmodernism, through a process of historical negation, attempted to date all that has preceded it, particularly, the more immediately antecedental high modernism, by making nonsense of essence (and if you like sense of nonsense); by denying foundation and pronouncing the sovereignty of individual intellectual space, by defying consensual rationality, hierarchy and order, as universal systems in thought. History ceased to exist except as individualized renditions and interpretations of experience. In short "everything goes". While Appiah confesses that he has no definition of postmodernism, his catalogue of attributes which project the postmodernist syndrome (p.231) serve better than a definition, and in spite of his critical divorce from Habermas, Lyotard and Jameson, his observations point firmly to the fact that postmodernism is a legitimate child of western modernism, and that it bears the birthmarks and genetic fingerprint of its parentage.

This history of changing Euro-centric intellectual fashions cannot be understood outside the context of the social and economic fortunes of western society. They are as much reflections of late capitalism as they are the articulation of dominant groups and ideas of our times in western society. It is the contemporary philosophy of the controlling voices of one corner of the world narcisstically looking at itself and dismissively contemplating the rest of us. Postmodernism cannot, and does not, transcend *wissensoziologie* however much it presses verbal ingenuity into its own service. Ideas and views do not descend on us like manna from heaven. They have social, historical, economic and cultural derivations. Last but not least, they have serious political implications. If everything goes, everything is justified, and its each for himself and the good lord for us all. We need to remind ourselves that ideas are born in space and time, and die, in space and time. Like the trendy fashions which have preceded it, the demise of the postmodernist position is inevitable, and I dare say historically this is probably just round the corner. In a recent conversation with the Norwegian anthropologist Lief Manger, he remarked that during recent attendances of meetings of the American Anthropological Association he has perceived a gradual shift from individualized narratives to searches for common perceptions.

Of Race, Race-men and Men

Away from his flighty forays into the postmodernist universe and space, Appiah makes many happy landings, and some bumpy ones too. He demeans Pan-Africanism with a selective logic of factual emphasis punctuated by equally factual silences, which in sum add up to the distortions he wishes to avoid. The triumph of Pan-Africanist anti-colonialism ends up as a racist monster conceived and weaned in the diaspora:

> ... what bound those African-American and Afro-Caribbean Pan-Africanists together was the partially African ancestry they shared, and since that ancestry mattered in the New World through its various folk-theories of race, a racial understanding of their solidarity was, perhaps, an inevitable development; and this was reinforced by the fact that a few crucial figures - Nkrumah among them - had travelled in the opposite direction to Crummell, seeking education in the black colleges of the United States. The tradition on which the francophone intellectuals of the post-war era drew, whether articulated by Aime Cesaire, from the New World, or Leopold Senghor from the Old, shared the European and American view of race. Like Pan-Africanism, *negritude* begins with the assumption of the racial solidarity of the Negro (p.6).

Subsumed in the belly of western culture, neither Senghor nor Cesaire could have escaped the dominant conceptions of race prevalent in their times, which enjoyed the blessing of some of the most acknowledged authorities on the question. It never was an issue of any centrality in their concerns, except in their populist constructions and summations of the essence of an experience which is non-western in foundation, which defines the African as representative of that experience, and which attempts to accord the African as a historical representative, respect for those features of history and culture which show the African off as different from the westerner. Not only because the African is culturally different from the westerner, but also because the westerner has always regarded him/herself as different from everybody else. What bound those African-American and Afro-Caribbean Pan-Africanists was of course the African ancestry they shared, but only because of the wider societal implications that fact underscored. People who share that ancestry were, and in some instances, are still faced with a colour-bar, everywhere they live with whites. Whether the intensity of this discrimination differed is another matter; the key fact is that people of African ancestry suffered bitterly everywhere they lived with whites, what V.G. Kiernan in his *The Lords of Humankind* described as the "aura of slavery" has hung around people of African ancestry.

If black people came together, they did not do this simply to celebrate, worship or glorify their colour; they got together to organize ways and means of overthrowing the economic, political and cultural burden and oppression which white people had imposed on them, and which was rationalized by their oppressors in the name of colour. Colour consciousness has been thrust on blacks by whites. In the joint experience of black and white, it is the social power of the latter which has determined the conditions of coexistence of black and white.

Appiah writes that, in the post-Second World War world, Europe-based Africans, students and former students for the most;

> who went home to create postcolonial Africa did not need to discuss or analyze race. It was the notion that had bound them together in the first place. The lesson the Africans drew from the Nazis - indeed from the Second World War as a whole - was not the danger of racism but the falsehood of the opposition between a humane

European "modernity" and the "barbarism" of the non-white world. We had known that European colonialism could lay waste African lives with a careless ease; now we knew that white people could take the murderous tools of modernity and apply them to each other (p.6).

Africans knew this well before the Second World War. Soldiers from the French African colonies had fought in Europe and seen the slaughter of trench warfare and European internecine bloodletting. In his biographical reconstruction of the life of the legendary Senegalese boxer *Battling Siki, Het Levensverhaal van M'Barick Fal*, Albert Stol evokes the war front conditions of African soldiers: "Day and night, they were under artillery fire, the *zi pan-pan* as they called it. Regularly they would rush out of the trenches forward over the dead bodies of their earlier killed comrades, in order to attack the enemy" (2). The real lesson Africans took from the Second World War was that unlike what had happened during the First World War in which they fought for the freedom of their colonial masters without tangible post-war results for themselves, this time, they should have their own freedom; freedom from colonial rule. Of course, despite rampant racism in Europe, Africans and all other people from the Third World till today, have always discovered warm, open-minded and humane people amongst Europeans. There is an Akan saying that, *kro bia ra, Kwesi wo mu*, literally every town/village has Kwesis (Kwesi being a common name). The extended meaning of this is that good and bad people are everywhere. I can also unequivocally confirm "warm memories of European friends" (p.7), but that does not deny the overwhelming racism of life in the west for black people. It is said of Kobina Sekyi, the famous African nationalist, that in on his way to the UK for legal education,

> ... he returned to England in late 1915 on the *S.S. Falaba* in company with some fellow students. It was while the ship was in the Irish Sea that it was torpedoed by a German U-Boat; some lives were lost, but Sekyi managed to clamber on to a life boat. According to interviews with some of his surviving friends in Cape Coast, it was this incident that finally convinced Sekyi that African

values and interests were incompatible with those of Europe. I was informed by those to whom he wrote after the incident that after he had just managed to get into a lifeboat one of the Europeans started shouting at him to get off, as he (Sekyi) a black man, had no right to be alive when whites were drowning. In the view of some of those I interviewed, this was the traumatic experience that finally led Sekyi (to use the title of one of his unpublished manuscripts) to "the parting of ways". His next three years in Britain, therefore, were as far as he was concerned merely "the lucid interval sustained" (3).

During my student days in the Netherlands, I recall an old secondary school friend from Ghana who as a result of racist conditions, almost developed paranoia to the point where, when we walked on the street and he saw people (not in the least concerned with us) laughing and walking in the opposite side of the street, he would gently butt me in the side saying, "look, look, they are laughing at us".

We cannot solve the problem of western racism by molly coddling it, or failing to look it straight in the face. It would be quite true to say that racism as known by the African in the USA was more openly and directly vicious, than was, or has been experienced, on most of the African continent or the West Indies; places where the African has always been in the majority. But it is important to remember that it was only a matter of degree. In a great deal, if not over half the expanse of black Africa where Belgian, Portuguese and settler colonialism held sway the situation was never better or substantially different. When Patrice Lumumba as part of his speech (30th June 1960) opening the independence of The Congo (present-day Zaire), in the presence of the Belgian king Baudouin ringingly asserted: "From today we are no longer your *Makak* (Monkeys)" (4). He was cathartically setting the record straight with respect to his own feelings and his understanding of the feelings of his compatriots.

Appiah writes of western-educated Africans that:

> Since they came from cultures where black people were in the majority and where lives continued to be largely controlled by indigenous moral and cognitive conceptions, they had no reason to

believe that they were inferior to white people and they had correspondingly, less reason to resent them. This fact is of crucial importance in understanding the psychology of postcolonial Africa.... the experience of the vast majority of these citizens of Europe's African colonies was one of essentially shallow penetration by the colonizer (pp.7-8).

He is overstating his case. For one thing, one has got to make a difference of sorts between the African elite and the masses. In my understanding of the situation, both these categories of Africans have been affected by the poison of inferior self-perceptions, but in different ways. Although the elite is more grounded (than their African-American counterparts who in as far as African culture is concerned have been almost totally effaced) in African culture and is psychologically more protected from the ravages of colonially induced cultural self-denial, most quietly accept the superiority of western culture and see immersion in this, away from their roots, as a means of assuring social and economic elevation. One becomes christian and abjures "heathen and primitive practices" including Zionist and Ethiopian churches; one must endeavour to speak English or French like the Englishman or Frenchman; one must send his or her children to English-medium or French schools and universities if one can afford it; in a restaurant "continental" food (i.e. European food) is better than native food; to become a member of the *French Academy* is the ultimate emblem of scholastic triumph; if you studied in Europe or North America, you are a cut above those who studied in Africa, you are a "been-to" (you have been to Europe); the lighter your skin the better you are and there is a marked display of preference for lightskinned ladies among the men. It is unpleasant to raise these matters, but this must be done because the tragedy is that these realities persist. In a sane world, we should all marry whoever we will. Lord Learie Constantine's general observations of this latter attitude amongst black people is in my view tellingly correct. In his study, *Colour Bar*, he writes:

The tendency of coloured people (*black people*) to admire or to marry other coloured people of a lighter shade has been put forward

167

by some as an argument that coloured people themselves admit a dislike of dark skins, and by inference agree that a white person who marries a black one is accepting an inferior as mate. But in fact it is easily apparent that this frequent desire to "marry lighter" is an instinctive attempt to escape from the *economic* and *social* penalties suffered by a black person in a white community. In a black community in its native setting, as among Negro tribes in Central Africa, there is no wish to marry the white women explorers who sometimes penetrate those areas. Far from it, they are generally considered by tribesmen as lean, ugly and unattractive compared with local women (5).

In as far as the African elite is concerned, these values are more unspoken than spoken. Many will in argument or discussion squeamishly deny them, but our practice speaks truthful volumes on this. It seems to me that whichever way you look at it, these attitudes and values are those of people who find their own inferior. The African masses are more tradition-bound and are more grounded in their own time-confirmed world. But they live with an elite, a reference group of dominant classes which are obviously aspiring to the cultural world of Europeans, in spite of their numerous denials. They see their own children and kinsmen leave the comforts and discomforts of traditional life for the more economically and socially rewarding ways of the west, and have over the years become slowly convinced that - *Wu yi nyame a, obroni na eba* - the white man is next in line to god. There was a joke circulating in Ghana some years ago, during the 1970s to be precise, that an illiterate farmer said to his mate "if you are going to church on a Sunday, and you run into a white person, you can as well go home, because you have met god".

There is certainly much more confidence in indigenous culture and customary usages amongst the masses, much more trust and resilience in the value of their own cultural heritage amongst the masses, but this is constantly being challenged by the example of an elite which ceaselessly turns it back on its roots; a captured elite, castrated by western cultural overkill. The point I am making here is clearly at variance with Appiah's contention that:

To insist in these circumstances on the alienation of (Western) educated colonials, on their incapacity to appreciate and value their own traditions, is to risk mistaking both the power of this primary experience and the vigour of many forms of cultural resistance to colonialism. A sense that the colonisers overrate the extent of their cultural penetration is consistent with anger or hatred or a longing for freedom; but it does not entail the failures of self-confidence that lead to alienation (p.9)

When the African child in a French colony read a book telling him or her about "our ancestors" the Gauls, the cultural assault was relentless and the psychological damage inestimable. Decades of education which has persistently glorified everything the westerner has represented at home and in Africa has definitely left feelings of inferiority in many Africans. Pushing back this legacy is no mean task especially if the elite which must lead the counter attack is diffident and confused or lacks resolute determination. I would argue that certainly, the match has not been lost, and would like even to assert that the match will not be lost.

There is enough baggage and muscle in African culture to hold its own in the long run, but, that is possible, if and only if, a counter-elite emerges in the coming years which realizes the shattering effect of colonial culture on us and which is able to roll back the effects of indiscriminate cultural assimilation, and is able to recentre the African cultural inheritance at the heart of the African development project and treats cultural borrowing as adaptable additions and not wholesale replacements of our heritage. We do well to remember the Asian experience, in this respect taking a page out of Mao Tse Tung's book, and reminding ourselves that China today with a growth rate of twelve percent per annum over a decade, is the fastest growing economy in the world. We are entering the next millennium under Asian economic leadership. In 1956, in a talk to Music Workers, he suggested that,

The Western things which you study are useful, but you should master both Western and Chinese things, and should not "completely Westernize". You should devote attention to Chinese things, do your utmost to study and develop them, with the aim of creating our own

Chinese things with characteristic national form and style. If you grasp this basic policy your work will have a great future (6).

Kwame Appiah's definitional analysis of race and racialism is one of the finest areas of his work. His superb analytical equipment comes fully to life. His distinction between extrinsic and intrinsic racism is engaging and bristles with the display of eloquent analytical techniques but they are not without problems. My first and general problem with his analysis here is its excessive formalism and subjectivism. There is hardly any difficulty with his formulation of racialism; the idea that, ... "that there are heritable characteristics, possessed by members of our species, which allow us to divide them into a small set of races, in such a way that all the members of these races share certain traits and tendencies with each other that they do not share with members of any other race" (p.18). He is easily able to make mince meat of this bogus and discredited argument and adequately exposes its scientific ineptitude in his chapter on the *Illusions of Race*.

It is in the definitions of extrinsic and intrinsic racism and their interpenetrative space that further difficulties arise. Appiah writes that "extrinsic racists make moral distinctions between members of different races because they believe that the racial essence entails certain morally relevant qualities. The basis for the extrinsic racist's discrimination between people is their belief that members of different races differ in respects that *warrant* the differential treatment". Extrinsic racists for Appiah are sometimes able to change their views in the face of "evidence that there are no such differences in morally relevant characteristics". At this juncture, Appiah's thinking becomes woolly and nebulous. He continues; "if the racist is sincere - what we have is no longer a false doctrine but a cognitive incapacity". How does this cognitive incapacity arise, what does it consist of, what are its sociological groundings? At this point, the whole problem becomes one of sentiment, cognitive ability or disability or even feeble-mindedness.

In spite of the fact that Appiah recognizes that such cognitive discrepancies constitute types of false consciousness and could for example be related to conditions of privilege or underprivilege, in other words positions in the structures of production, distribution and exchange, he at this point backs off from the probe and announces: "My business here is not with the psychological or (perhaps more importantly) the social process by which these defences operate.." (p.20). Just as the inquiry becomes interesting he fights shy, and despite his claim of avoiding psychological dissections, he lapses into psychologism and suggests that "an inability to change your mind in the face of evidence is a cognitive incapacity; it is one that all of us surely suffer from in some areas of belief". Sincerity and insincerity and undefined areas of belief cannot be serious points of philosophical inquiry. He partly redeems his thinking by observing that "it would be odd to call someone brought up in a remote corner of the world with false and demeaning views about white people a racist if he or she gave up these beliefs quite easily in the face of evidence". Such people are more importantly ignorant and uninformed, and the world has millions of them.

Intrinsic racists are for Appiah, "people who differentiate morally between members of different races, because they believe that each race has a different moral status, quite independent of the characteristics that its members share. Just as, for example, many people assume that the bare fact that they are biologically related to another person - a brother, an aunt, a cousin - gives them a moral interest in that person, so an intrinsic racist holds that the bare fact of being of the same race is a reason for preferring one person to another" (p.21). Linking these two formulations of types of racism, he attenuates the borders of the two categories to create an interpenetrative space by hinging the problem on "sincerity" and "insincerity": "...the sincere extrinsic racist may suffer from a cognitive incapacity. But some who espouse extrinsic racist doctrines are simply insincere intrinsic racists" (p.21). The simple upshot of these specious ratiocinations and also unfortunately sometimes "trivial logic-chopping" (p.176) reads; "the fundamental difference between intrinsic and extrinsic racism is that the former declares some group objectionable, no matter what its traits, while the latter founds its dislikes in allegations about objectionable characteristics" (p.22). Unfortunately, none of it is convincing, and in spite of its considerable verbal flourishes, it is a subjective logical process based on conceptual quicksand, and obliquity of judgement.

In as far as Crummell held the language and culture of the westerner in the highest regard and considered the language and culture of native Africans in whose name he claimed to speak in the lowest regard, he shares a lot with the mind-set of those elites of African descent who have a poor estimation of the weakly "acculturated" Africa. If we agree to Appiah's formulations it is easy to classify Crummell's views as racist. But as Appiah also rightly points out: "Part of our resistance, therefore to calling the racial views of Crummell by the same term that we use to describe the attitudes of many Afrikaners surely resides in the fact that Crummell never for a moment contemplated using race as a basis for inflicting harm" (p.25). But, here again, Appiah provides us with some indigestible philosophical fare.

The history and experience of institutionalized racism in South Africa - apartheid - has been deeply anti-human, pernicious in the extreme and "inflicted harm". It was not only Afrikaners who were centrally responsible for its practice, but rather whites in general, although Afrikaners within the dominant classes were mainly in the leadership of its policy formulation and practice. None of the ideologues of Apartheid ever admitted that the policy of what they preferred to call "separate development" was intended to "inflict harm". For the apartheid ideologues and apologists, if the system inflicted harm, it was unintended. This is the argument which F.W. De Klerk the leader of the National Party (the party which created apartheid) made recently (September 1996) in his submission to the Truth Commission instituted to look into the crimes of apartheid. True enough, it "inflicted harm" and grievous harm at that. The crux of the matter is that racism in the real sense of the term defines a social relationship. It is within social structures that racism comes alive. No discussion of racism properly engages reality until it makes historical landing and is socially and economically grounded. It is this key aspect of the question which is neglected or poorly articulated in Appiah's exciting work.

Crummell and Du Bois were not race theoreticians or ideologues in the sense in which Gobineau, Grant or Chamberlain were. However theoretically susceptible and racist-prone some of their ideas were, at heart their racial rationalisations were attempts to assert their humanity in the face of the indignities and inferior "racial status" which others defined for people of their kind.

There is hardly any thinker of the period whose ideas on race were not racist, seen with the benefit of hindsight. Inadequate science and poorly crafted defensive rhetorical postures lie at the heart of their theoretical obfuscations. Taken seriously, Appiah's diagnosis of racism applies to all pre-20th century thought on race and a good deal of 20th century thinking. If this includes some of the assumptions of Crummell and Du Bois, as it very well does, fair enough. Better comparative evidence of the generalized and universal character of racist thought in contemporary social and political philosophy would have enabled Appiah's text to achieve balance and would have done justice to his work. Because of the relative historical decontextualization of the presentation of the philosophically racist features of the work of Du Bois and Crummell, his discourse in this respect lapses into an exercise in victimization. In effect, the ideologues of the victims of racism come across as principal pillars in racist ideology. Although thinkers like Hume and the jingoist propagandist Tupper bring up contrasting faces, these come across rather weakly. Comparative racist ideas in the work of figures like, J.A. Froude, Charles Dilke, Rudyard Kipling, H.S. Grogan, Joseph Chamberlain, Walter Bagehot, Winston Churchill and Alexander Cadogan would have helped to reveal the ubiquitousness of manifest and latent racist ideology.

I have, elsewhere in this book, drawn attention to Churchill's loudly racist language: "America should be temperate and wise about taking time to solve its Negro problem. After all, you can't take twenty million of them into your belly just like that. Nonsense to say that the black is the same as the white" (7). Sir Alexander Cadogan, in his diaries, writes "we tell the Russians everything and play square with them. They are the most stinking creepy set of Jews I've ever come across" (Monday, 17th January, 1944) (8). Appiah's grandfather, returning to Britain early in 1942 from Moscow, where for about two years he had served as British Ambassador, became Lord Privy Seal and Leader of the House of Commons. In a memorandum of the 12th October 1942, prepared for Cabinet it is noted:

> Cripps ended by offering several pieces of advice, not so far removed from Dowler's conclusions but phrased a little more circumspectly. The first point was: "Be friendly and sympathetic towards coloured American Troops - but avoid intimate relationships". Secondly: "If you find yourselves in the company of white and coloured troops.... make it your business to avoid unpleasantness. It is much the best, however, to avoid such situations". The third point raised the old taboo: "It is undesirable that a white woman should go about *alone* in the company of a coloured American..."(9).

Even the venerable Marx and his other intellectual half Engels have not been exempt from the prejudices of their age. While in the view of Chaloner and Henderson, Engels was not as smitten by the virus of racist fixation as Marx was, he was also a carrier of the virus. Regarding Marx our attention has for example been drawn to a letter he wrote to Engels relating largely to Ferdinand Lassalle in 1862. Ferdinard Lassalle, who was a Jew from Breslau in Silesia, as a young man had led the workers of Dusseldorf during the revolution of 1848. But he had never been a member of the Communist League. Although Marx saw the need to cooperate with Lassalle, his views on him to his friend Engels was not as clean as one would have guessed. When Lassalle was Marx's guest in London in 1862, Marx wrote to Engels:

> It is now perfectly clear to me that, as the shape of his head and the growth of his hair indicate, he is descended from the negroes who joined in the flight of Moses from Egypt (unless his mother or grandmother on the father's side was crossed with a nigger). Now this union of Jewishness to Germanness on a negro basis was bound to produce an extraordinary hybrid. The importunity of the fellow is also niggerlike (10).

Few of Marx' uncountable admirers are aware of the fact that he was not with regards to racist sentiments totally free from the prejudices of Europe of his times. This of course does not distract from his enormous contribution to the theory and practice of revolution as an instrument for the emancipation of the depressed classes of our times. Chaloner and Henderson make the point that in spite of the tell-tale signs of racist baggage that can be found in Engels' output;

> Just as Engels rarely showed any antipathy towards the Jews, so he had no prejudices against coloured peoples. He rejected the view commonly expressed by explorers and missionaries in his day that native peoples were "heathen savages" who were obviously inferior to white races (11).

Racist utterances litter the expressions of many western leaders of mind and action, right into the 20th century (12). If on the basis of such expressions, analyses of the thought and philosophies of these figures are conducted without proper historical and contextual situation, many would appear in very questionable stature.

Caliban's Prospects

His chapter, *Old Gods, New Worlds* raises very important issues crucial to any attempt by us as Africans in general to put feelings of historical and cultural inferiority behind us. Although his treatment of important anthropological minds like Geertz, Levi-Strauss, and Durkheim is perfunctory and superficial, the final destination of the discussion in this chapter is of great interest. Durkheim, in particular who is given short shrift, deserves better treatment. What Durkheim's proto-functionalist sociology, specifically in his *The Elementary Forms of Religious Life,* teaches which is of relevance to us here, is that religion and ritual are institutions for social cohesion and moral order. Religion and ritual emerge as soon as there is a separation between the sacred and the profane, but since things are not sacred or profane on account of inherent qualities but purely human designation, it is arguable that the demystification of the sacred, the world of invisible agents, is possible if the utilitarian considerations of the case are forceful enough.

175

Let us start with the terminal parts of this presentation which sit uncomfortably. Appiah writes: "Most Africans, now, whether converted to Islam or Christianity or not, still share the beliefs of their ancestors in an ontology of invisible things" (p.218). Further on he adds: "These beliefs in invisible agents mean that most Africans cannot fully accept those scientific theories in the West that are inconsistent with it. ... If modernisation is conceived of in part as the acceptance of science, we have to decide whether we think the evidence obliges us to give up the invisible ontology" (p.219).

It seems to me that implicit in this discourse is the assumption that the world of invisible agents and that of science and modernization are oppositional realities. There is a popular contemporary western school of social science concerned with issues of development projects in the Third World which also talks in terms of "cultural blockages", which are considered to be institutional forms in the cultural world of preindustrial Third World societies preventing the adoption of scientific innovations and practices necessary for the transformation of these societies. Both the theoreticians of "cultural blockages" and Appiah appear to me to be misunderstanding the nature of the problem. It would seem to me, that the world of invisible agents and that of modern science and technology are in an important sense actually different points on a continuum, which involves the way we perceive and act upon the external world (and for some its invisible extensions). In preindustrial societies (historically these have from the vantage point of the present been largely precapitalist) the instruments of mediation and intervention have been materially spare and technologically poorly differentiated. The historical gradient of this technological differentiation as we move along the continuum, is paralleled by changing degrees of evolving linguistic complexity. Labour as an expression of the intervention process defines the basis of social praxis. It is through social praxis and the cumulative results of this that the process of disinhabiting the world of invisible things and the movement into the scientific world is achieved.

Years ago, in 1977 to be precise, I asked the Chinese intellectual Chen Yi Fei how this problem is tackled in China. His response was, that in the treatment of, for example, sick people in rural China, it is the repetitive results of efficacious scientific demonstrations in preventive and curative practice which change the views of peasants and help them to shed belief in the world of invisible things. We need to culturally carry our own as we march into the brave new world of science and technology, but as we do this, we must relentlessly discard the perishable cultural cargo that we carry along the way, as and when this is necessary.

We cannot move forward successfully if we throw all our belongings away as the narrator of Ake Loba's creation suggests. I however share Appiah's calculation that "in this area we can learn together with other cultures - including, for example, the Japanese culture which has apparently managed a certain segregation of moral-political and cognitive spheres" (p.220). But how have they done this? By building on their own, but freely importing and adapting whatever else from outside enriches what they have (13).

The western paradigm needs to be closely examined, for even here the world of superstition and invisible things has survived much of what is on the surface a rugged scientific and technological culture. Westerners, till today, including some of their best scientists and technologists, at church on Sundays during communion, symbolically eat the body of Christ and drink his blood, through a ritual eating of bread and drinking of wine respectively. The doctrine of immaculate conception lives on.

The Vacancy of African Philosophy

One of the best, or possibly the best chapter in Appiah's book is *Ethnophilosophy and its Critics*. Here he is indubitably on *terra firma*. There is hardly a paragraph which is not strikingly lucid. Appiah looks closely at Paulin Hountondji's idea of ethnophilosophy which grapples with the problem of demarcating a claim to philosophical activity in Africa by Africans in the past and present. He questions the use of Hountondji's idea of conceptualizing African philosophy as "a set of texts, specifically the set of texts written by Africans themselves and described as philosophical by their authors themselves". On the one hand Appiah finds this too restrictive in the sense that it has to be written, on the other hand he also rightly asks if this is meant to suggest that the issue can be settled by "definitional fiat" (p.136). He prefers the consideration and inclusion of folk-philosophy.

Within the ambit of folk-philosophy the areas of concern of western philosophy are also reflected. Appiah writes;

> the important questions for African scholars about their involvement with western academic philosophy are not to be settled by facts of geography. For they will want to ask, first, if there is anything distinctive they can bring to the western tradition from their history and culture, their languages and traditions, and, second, what, in Africa, is the teaching and writing of western-style philosophy for ....(p.144).

Starting from Placide Tempels' foundational work in ethnophilosophy, he interweaves his discussion with the views of Kwasi Wiredu, Ben Oguah, Helaine Minkus, John Ayoade, Kwame Gyekye, and Marcien Towa. Appiah is thoroughly consistent in this chapter and warns against a simple projection of western ideas while comparatively interrogating them. He writes:

> For if philosophers are to contribute - at the conceptual level - to the solution of Africa's real problems then they need to begin with a deep understanding of the traditional conceptual worlds the vast majority of their fellow nationals inhabit. In this, I believe, it is Wiredu who is right: what is wrong with the ethnophilosophers is that they have never gone beyond this essentially preliminary step. "The test," Wiredu says, "of a contemporary African philospher's conception of African philosophy is whether it enables him to engage fruitfully in the activity of modern philosophising with an African conscience". (p.170).

An African conscience is difficult to conceive of without historical and cultural baggage. In Appiah's flight from these difficulties he ends up in the embrace of Wiredu. Wiredu makes explicit the connection between an understanding of tradition and his concern for the possibilities of modernization: "Obviously it is of prime philosophical importance to distinguish between traditional, pre-scientific thought and modern, scientific thought by means of a clearly articulated criterion or set of criteria" (p.167). I would argue that actually, "traditional thought" and "modern scientific thought" are not sharply distinguishable; like day and night they flow into each other. The more we move into the day, the more the features of the night are shed. There is no point at which elements of one condition are totally excluded from the composition of historical reality. This is why there can never be a time when scientific knowledge as a cumulative social fund reaches an absolute in societal expression. This is simply in the dialectical nature of things.

It seems to me, that one of the problems facing philosophers preoccupied with African concepts is the need to reckon with the periodization of concepts, and how such concepts relate to the ethnographic proximity of African cultural sub-sets, on the ground. Folk-philosophies as systems do not move through time unchanged. Indeed, the differences different concepts or notions reflect in meaning are tied to social and material changes in the evolution of these societies as social formations. In this sense, I would share Hountondji's view that, "the development of philosophy is in some way a function of the development of the sciences" (p.169).

There is another area to which attention also needs to be directed. This is the area of the history of ideas of Africans about African society. A. Ayo Langley's introduction to *Ideologies of Liberation in Black Africa; 1856-1970* is only a superficial starter. Claude Wauthier's *The Literature and Thought of Modern Africa* rich and exciting as it is does not sufficiently mill the material and does not regard philosophical analysis thereof as an issue of central concern. Equally devoid of a pure philosophical focus are Robert July's *The Origins of Modern African Thought* and Henry Wilson's (ed.) *Origins of West African Nationalism*. Wilson's is the least digested of the lot, and is largely restricted to four countries in English-speaking West Africa. Africans have been grappling with questions of social and political philosophy relating to Africa for some time now, and synthetic work which unites or disunites these works is overdue.

Ultimately, if we want to move forward, we must gain control over knowledge production and knowledge about ourselves and our

179

societies. Thinking Africans are tired of the insulting idea that others know and understand them better than they understand themselves. It is all well and good to argue that knowledge is indeed a universal fund, but in the real world, no society moves forward if "the best authorities" about that society are located in other societies and other cultures. That sort of situation is in fact a colonial, or for our purposes, in our times, a neocolonial situation. Any philosophical position which implicitly or explicitly acquiesces in that mental frame perpetuates and extends African inferiority and subordination.

Can Africans understand themselves through the agency of other peoples' languages? Here again, my view is that only limitedly is this possible. We need to make African languages carry philosophy. We need to understand Plato and ourselves in our own languages. Only then can we develop with confidence with our historical baggage and culture.

The interpenetration of the keywords, decolonisation, authenticity, identity, language, tradition and culture are interestingly problematized in relation to the work of writers like Soyinka and Achebe, Ngugi and Ouologuem. The discussions of Soyinka and Achebe are particularly rich and revealing.

> For Africa,.........though trained in Europe or in schools and universities dominated by European culture, the African writers' concern is not with the discovery of a self that is the object of an inner voyage of discovery. Their problem - though not, of course, their subject - is finding a public role, not a private self. If European intellectuals, though comfortable inside their culture and traditions, have an image of themselves as outsiders, African intellectuals are uncomfortable outsiders, seeking to develop their cultures in directions that will give them a role (p.120).

The foundations of this problem lie in the language we use as writers. What audience do we define and address when we write in English and French, which cultures do we tap into? The road to "authenticity", in the way Appiah wants us to understand it, (as different from Mobutuism) cannot be reached in speech forms which lie outside the native cultural world of the writer.

Appiah goes on to say:

> For the relation of African writers to the African past is a web of delicate ambiguities. If they have learned neither to despise it nor try to ignore it - and there are many witnesses to the difficulty of this decolonisation of the mind - they have still to learn how to assimilate and transcend it (p.121).

But into which realm should African writers transcend? African writers should not simply assimilate their past and culture, they should own it, stand in it and use it, as a basis for contributing to the universal human fund. When Achebe writes that "It is, of course, true that the African identity is still in the making. There isn't a final identity that is African. But, at the same time, there is an identity coming into existence (Quoted on p.280)", he is attesting to the fluidity of the African identity (like all other identities in the world). Until Bismarck there were no Germans, as we know them now. There were Prussians, Bavarians, Hanoverians etc. The British include, Welsh, English, Scottish and Irish. All of these and more are Europeans who have often fought bitterly against each other and in some cases still do so. They were all Europeans in the 18th and 19th centuries, and are still Europeans. But, the substance of being a European today, a member of the European Community, is surely considerably different from what was the case in the early 19th century. To suggest as Appiah does that in the 19th century an African identity did not exist, but is appearing in the 20th century is undialectical. What is more correct to say is that being an African in the 19th century is different from what it is now. I would, likewise modify the Achebe quote by suggesting that, there is, and has been, an identity in existence but its character and substance is constantly changing. It is as much a self-recognition, a self-definition, as it is a definition of the African by others, although these two definitional roots and directions are not identical in intent or focus. When the Akan say *Obibrini*, they mean an African; *Abibriman* or blackman's country is nowhere but Africa. Those who for centuries, made it their activity to enslave and carry Africans across the Atlantic or into the Near East identified and knew very well who they were taking away.

The cultures and sub-cultures from which this African identity or identities are derived differ, but the cultural differences in Africa, for anybody who knows the continent and the people well, are narrow and narrower than Appiah realises. There is a great degree of structural affinity between African cultures, and enough that differentiates them as a set in relation to all the major cultures of the world. Within the identity Chinese, European, Arab or Indian, there are as many cultural differences as there are among Africans. To miss, or dismiss this, is to seriously misunderstand Africa and her peoples.

Appiah should have acknowledged his mother who made it her life's work to collect and catalogue Akan proverbs. Most of the proverbs reflected in the text are in all probability drawn from this source. The slogan of the United Nationalist Party, *Abaa ba sèi* (I have slightly altered the orthography), is Ga and not Akan.

In My Father's House is an outstanding piece of work. It is richly textured and eloquently argued. Appiah raises leading questions and offers many useful clues and answers. There are numerous other questions which flow out of his discourse. But, if as the bulk of the text does, interrogating and showing Pan-Africanism off as racism, then he has historically made a mountain out of a mole hill. 19th century, and a good part of 20th century philosophy, with regards to the matters dealt with in the text, was overwhelmingly racist. A good part of this racism was implicit, but not all, and based on poor scientific knowledge. None of the icons of Pan-Africanist thought was avowedly racist. While Pan-Africanism has carried its share of 19th century ignorance and racist theoretical confusion, it has never in practice, anywhere, been practically anti-human. On the contrary it has been the main ideological vehicle for the emancipation of people of African descent since its early beginnings. Unless both sides of the story are put into proper perspective in any discussion of the idea and its practice, it is very easy to fall into the sort of argumentation where the historical victims of western (and this happens to be white) racism, and the prime ideologues of the little freedom we have seen this century, are made to appear in bad light. We must be careful not to accuse the victims, in father's house.

Notes

1. F. R. Leavis. *The Living Principle: "English" as a Discipline of Thought*. London. 1975. Quoted here from Roy Fuller. *The Survival of Dr. Leavis. Bearing Reality. Encounter. December 1975*. pp. 65-66.

2. Albert Stol. *Battling Siki. Het Levensverhaal van M'Barick Fal*. Amsterdam. 1991. p.50.

3. See, J. Ayo Langley's Introduction to Kobina Sekyi. *The Blinkards*. London. 1974, 1982 edition, p.7.

4. See, Colin Legum's foreword. In, Patrice Lumumba. *Congo My Country*. London. 1962.

5. See, Learie Constantine. *Colour Bar*. London. 1954. p.93.

6. Quoted here from, Stuart Schram. *Mao Tse Tung Unrehearsed. Talks and Letters; 1956-1971*. Harmondsworth. 1974. p.90.

7. C. L. Sulzberger. *The Last of the Giants*. London. 1972. pp.302-303.

8. David Dilks (ed). *The Diaries of Sir Alexander Cadogan*. 1938-1945. London. 1971. p.597.

9. Graham Smith. *When Jim Crow met John Bull. Black American Soldiers in World War 11 Britain*. London. 1987. p.75-76.

10. Marx to Engels, 30 July 1862. In, Marx-Engels, *Gesamtausgabe, Part iii, Vol 3*, pp. 82-84. On Marx as "at once a racialist himself and the cause of racialism in others', see George Watson, *The English Ideology* (1973), p.211. Quoted here from W.H. Chaloner and W.O. Henderson. Marx/Engels and Racism. *Encounter. July 1975*. p.19.

11. Ibid. p.21.

12. Nancy Cunard, daughter of Lady Emerald and Sir Bache Cunard the shipping magnate attracted the approbium of the British upper classes for her intense associations with black people (including George Padmore and a host of other African nationalists). Lady Oxford, Margot Asquith is reported on an occasion to have remarked to Emerald Cunard; ".....well, Maud, what's Nancy up to now? Is it dope, drink or niggers". The conductor Sir Thomas Beecham was of the view that Nancy "should be tarred and feathered". When Nancy inquired from the writer George Moore if he entertained any colour prejudice, "after careful deliberation", his

response was, "No ... I think none, but the subject has never come my way. You see, I've never known anyone of colour, not even an Indian. I have met neither a brown man, nor yet a black man. I do not believe I could get on well with a black man, my dear. I think the best I could manage would perhaps be a yellow man". See, Daphne Fielding. *Emerald and Nancy. Lady Cunard and her Daughter*. London. 1968. pp.104-105. The last quote can also be found in, Nancy Cunard. *Black Man and White Ladyship, An Anniversary*. Toulouse. 1931.

13. Tatsuo Kawai. *The Goal of Japanese Expansion*. Tokyo. 1938. pp.35-50.

INDEX

Decraene, Phillippe 73, 95
Deleuze, G. 162
Deng, William 99
Derrida 162
Desta, Makonnen 22
Dilke, Charles 173
Diodorus, Siculus 147
Diop, Cheikh Anta 86, 144
Du Bois, David 104, 106
Du Bois, W.E.B. 22, 24, 36, 50, 51,
    62, 72-81, 84, 95-97, 156, 172, 173
Du Plessis, L.L. 120, 121, 136, 137
Durkheim, Emile 150, 175
Duse, Mohammed Ali 48
Eads, Brian 106
Ellis, Jimmy 131
Esterhuyse, Jan 121, 137
Evans-Pritchard, E. 150
Fafunwa, Babatunde 92, 97
Fal, M'barick 165, 183
Fanon, Frantz 1, 2, 14, 25, 41, 112, 143
Farrakhan, Louis 104, 108
Fichte, Johann Gottlieb 77
Forde, D. 150
Foreign native 58
Fortes, Meyer 150
Foucault, M. 143, 152, 162
Froude, J.A. 173
Gallieni, Joseph 79
Garang, John 98
Garvey, Marcus 21, 26, 50, 72, 84, 95
Gbatala, Ali 19
Geertz, Clifford 175
Geiss, Immanuel 73, 95, 102, 104
Gerwel, Jakes 121, 137
Ghana-Guinea Joint Declaration 9
GHANASO 7, 60
Gillespie, Dizzy 160
Grant, Bernie 106
Griaule, Marcel 144
Grogan, H.S. 173
Gumplowicz, Ludwig 79
Gunther, John 119, 136

Gyekye, Kwame 178
Harris, J.E. 72, 95
Harris, Marvin 142, 143, 150, 154
Hegel, Greorg Wilhelm Friedrich 81
Heidegger, Martin 160
Henderson, W.O. 174, 175, 183
Herder, J.G. 77
Herodotus 147
Hesse, J.A. 119
Hinden, Rita 8
Hippocrates 76
Ho Chi Minh 65, 113
Hofmeyer, J.H. 118, 136
Hooker, J.R. 73, 74, 95, 96
Horton, Africanus Beale 85
Hountondji, Paulin 146, 154, 177, 179
International Negro Workers Conference
    104
Jackson, Jesse 105
James, C.L.R. 22, 49, 85
July, R 179
Juuk, Kuol Manyang 100
Kalibala 21
Karenga, Maulana 103
Karikari, Kwame 13
Kaye, Cab 85
Keleuljang, Sirr Anai 98
Kenyatta, Jomo 8, 22, 23, 25, 36, 50,
    84, 85, 112
Kerouac, Jack 160
Khaddafi, Muammar 13, 108, 109
Khalil, Abdulla 19, 23
Khedive of Egypt 18
Kierkegaard, Soren 160
Kiernan, V.G. 164
King 26, 104, 105, 166
Kingsley, Mary 49, 61
Kipling, Rudyard 173
Klu, Kofi 102, 103
Koinange, Peter Mbiyu 22
Kok, Adam 122
Kotze, Clement 116, 117
Kuye, John Williamson 49, 61

DATE DUE

OCT 0 4 2000		
JUL 0 5 2009		
		Printed in USA

HIGHSMITH #45230